THE RIVER FAL

A Historical Guide from Source to Sea

D. G. Wilson

PiXZ

Title page: A foreshortened view of King Harry Reach,
looking towards the main estuary of Carrick Roads.

Back cover: Detail from John Norden's map of Powder Hundred, c.1600.

First published in Great Britain in 2017

British Library Cataloguing-in-Publication Data
A CIP record for this title is available from the British Library

ISBN 978 0 85710 112 9

PiXZ Books
Halsgrove House, Ryelands Business Park,
Bagley Road, Wellington, Somerset TA21 9PZ
Tel: 01823 653777
Fax: 01823 216796
email: sales@halsgrove.com

An imprint of Halstar Ltd, part of the
Halsgrove group of companies
Information on all Halsgrove titles is
available at: www.halsgrove.com

Printed and bound in India by Parksons Graphics

Contents

Biographical Note on the Author

David Wilson has had many years of experience in amateur archaeology, local history studies and sailing traditional craft. He has previously published books on the history of the River Thames, including *The Thames, Record of a Working Waterway* and *The Victorian Thames*. Following a career as a Thames lock keeper he retired to Cornwall in 1997 and has since produced the booklet *The Mills of a Cornish Valley* and the books *Falmouth Haven* and *Maritime History of Falmouth*. He has got to know his subject intimately, while sailing on the estuary, exploring the Fal Valley, and studying the history of the river through topographical and documentary sources.

A Description of the Work

The Fal is known as a famous estuary on the south coast of Cornwall, busy with shipping for hundreds of years. The river itself is perhaps less well known, but nevertheless its rural course is full of great historical interest. The objective of this book is to bring that history to the eyes of all those who love the Cornish countryside.

The river is described from its source above the wild beauty of Goss Moor, down to where it meets the main estuary. The unique underlying geology has resulted in a fascinating varied terrain. The granite uplands were the source of tin and other metals from the Bronze Age almost to the present day. The same area has been exploited for its vast deposits of china clay, for the production of ceramics and paper making. Water from the Fal and its tributaries played a vital part in these industries.

Further down the valley the river flows through a landscape farmed for thousands of years, resulting in a picturesque pattern of fields on the valley sides and rich meadows on the flood plain. Within the landscape human settlements vary from Iron Age hill forts to villages dating from medieval times.

Water-mills along the course of the river were vital for corn milling and industrial purposes. Using fieldwork and early documents the author has researched the histories of these, and of the villages of Grampound, Ruan Lanihorne and Tregony, discussing the work of earlier writers. His photographs have been chosen to complement the text and to feature aspects of the valley's natural environment.

Acknowledgements

Igive thanks to the number of people who have willingly assisted me during my research along the Valley of the Fal. They include John Yeo and Don Hallett at St Stephen, Steven Toms, Joy Floyd-Norris, Tina Tyler, and those whose names I unfortunately did not take: the Captain of the Melbur Works, and others at Trenowth, Golden and Tregony. Also members of the China Clay History Group; Royal Cornwall Polytechnic Society History Group. Staff at the Cornish Studies Library, Redruth and Cornwall Record Office, Truro. Dr Maryanne Kowaleski for her references to medieval shipping. John Muteham for technical assistance. Barbara Wilson for additional research. My special thanks to my wife, Roma, for her patience during our drives into the unknown, and for converting my scribblings into readable text.

Opposite:
The Map of
Cornwall, by
Joel Gascoyne,
1699.
Detail of the Fal
to Tregony from
its junction with
the Truro River.
Including the
tidal Tresillian
River.

S EARME
Stairefatt
Hanfouth
Nately
Nantelly
Trethurie
Nanfouth mill
Kelcoofe
Bedock
Tregue
Trabbus

THE HUND

Tregalfow
Trehane
Kuftean
Sparva
Trevifa
Tregel

Lanillie
Kallerrick
Polwhele
Trehover
Trenithon
Trevell
Corfufe

Bodrean
Lamellin
Tregofe

Penare ye higher
Tregorna
Trevean
Trucks

OF

PROBUS
Trewithan
Goldin
Tredin

Penare
Treliflian
Tinn Mills
Higens
bridg
Kalvofe

Trefimple
Carthon
Tregerrick
Treveras
Fee Water
Croger
Cary

MERTHER
Eglosmerther
Treworgy
CORNILLY
CUBY

Trevear
Tregage
Craft
Lellea
Penron
Tregor

Mopus
Line
Labradock
Trever

Trenian
Eenlongollen
S. Michael
PENKEVIL
Gear
Trewarthenick
Grigorie
Penrofe
Trevill

LEMORAN
RUAN=LINNI
Trethe
wy
Tredinnick
P

Tregothnan
Komble
Hugh Boscawin
Lemoran
Vernam
HORN
Crego
Demon
Horn
Caftle thems

Penkevill
Trelonk
Dern
Canithe
Trethilla
Tregifan
Patena
Tregooden
Tippett

Polmafk
ern
Devornvear
Trewiflan
Enaroofe
Trethege
Trelabifick

PHILLIGH
Treneflron
Ecclerrofe
Treworge
Treviles
Calleuder
Penfwage

Manick
Cregmullion
Treburras
Trefenhoufe

Couches
Shop
Wind mill
Perfew
Poropas
Calidrick
Trendenall
Trevifan
Tentove

ROSE
Treworthal
Penhallow
Mills
Trefufar
Treugfar
Creon

Treverras
Tredellams
Corfelick
Treworlas

Cowarton
Tregarewoon
Trenntham
Corgurell
Carne
VERIAN

LAND
Tregare
Villoholo
Rofevine
Mifcollan
Nare
Penee

Gunrounfon
Trerice
Lextoria
Kernoy
DENNI
Cheproys
Tregose
Kendra
Treth
Rosewin
Ilapean
Trelaner
Trevalkes
Treviscar
Belowsy
Kernick
Genamoras
Peritingate
Melida
Trethawser
Topaside
Tresvilla
Treneag
Gounabarne
Terris
Tregallans
Carloogus
Lowngate
Nakelly
Carwalfick
St STEPHENS
Nankelle
Trethurse
Fedock
Fall R
Bedeniek
Court Hey
Brannel
Bur
N D R E D
Sparva
Trenowith
Corlinnick
Trevisco
Trenithon
Trediniek
Penbetho
Tregellas
Nantellan
Tregose
Trevellan
GRAMPONT
Tremenhan
Teagues gate
Peng
Corfuse
Perrante
Luna
Trewithan
Lancarr
Triganjohn
Tenereek
Goldin
Tredinham
CREED
Trekenn
Reforla
Croger
Busue
Carveth
Trelewick
CUBY
Tregoning
Fenseouill
Rosewinn
Lower Trel
St Joseph
Tredinham
Voes
Luna
Lane va
Tregony
Polmarie
St ILVA
Trevill
Pengoose
Trevithick
Hicks
Trewise
Trelifick
Treworrack
Trevaskes
thew
wy
Tredinnick
P O W D E

Preface

The River Fal forms part of the catchment or drainage basin of the renowned Fal Estuary of West Cornwall. The river's southward course is contained in a landscape that varies in interest from dramatic to picturesque. From the time when much of Cornwall was covered in primordial forest, people have lived and worked here, in a valley sheltered from the four winds, clearing the land to create hill forts, farmsteads, mills, bridges, villages, castles and cornfields. Their labours have formed the valley we see today. The people of the Iron Age, or perhaps even from an earlier time, gave the river its name, the Fala; only they could have told us its meaning.

The source of the river, consisting of several springs, is at Pentivale, less than a mile to the south of the village of Roche and its well-known Rock, at an elevation of 200 metres above sea level. The springs, flowing with considerable volume, have carved out a deep narrow valley running to the northwest. The site is indicated by a single footpath post on the side of a minor road. Here the springs are hidden among a thicket of goat willow scrub and, in the summer, a profusion of invasive white-flowered Indian balsam. The rivulet first wanders westwards for several miles across Goss Moor, being augmented by streams from the waterlogged marsh, before turning southwards through the devastated, white dusted, landscape of china clay country. It runs in a deep channel through the Retew Gorge, seeming to be trying to avoid being associated with the immense opencast pits and waste tips on either side.

Below the bridge on the busy road to the west of St Stephen, the river flows through pleasant farming country before plunging 65 metres down through leafy Crowhill Gorge. The

Opposite:
The Map of Cornwall, by Joel Gascoyne, 1699. Detail of the Fal from Tregony, northwards towards the source.

9

The River Fal
at Golden.
The Iron Age
fort lies behind
the trees on top
of the hill.

dark mysterious Trenowth Wood, rising from its western flank, forms part of this very special site of scientific interest. The depth of the gorge, viewed from its southern end, is emphasised by the immense tall columns of the engineering masterpiece that is the viaduct of the Cornwall Railway. Down below, the alder-fringed river flows under a small road bridge before escaping again across open fields in a broadening valley.

Few roads run along the valley bottom, because the low flood plain can be inundated in winter. But views of the river, meandering across the meadows, might be obtained from the deep narrow lanes that traverse the slopes on either side, their banks clothed with primroses in springtime. Below Grampound the channel increases in volume, having been augmented by a few small tributaries, and the flood plain meadows become wider. Fine agricultural land covers the hills on either side, except where the slopes are too steep, when woodland takes over. The scenic views, over the ever-widening valley, continue to Tregony and beyond, until, after the flood plain is narrowed again by steep tree-clad hills, the river reaches sea level.

We walked on Golden Moor, midway between the river's source near Goss Moor, and to where it meets tidal waters below Ruan Lanihorne. Early maps and documents refer to the riverside meadows as Moors: Halbote Moor, Pomeroy Moor, and so on. The summer grass was short, temporarily used up, and the cattle had been taken off. Their dried calling cards indicated their former presence. These were interspersed by a few chalky-white mole hills; why were they white? The river murmered in its deep narrow channel, unseen behind a screen of tall alder trees. At their foot, on a piece of rough ground out of reach of the cattle, flowered meadowsweet and hemp agrimony. Their blooms were attracting insects, even a couple of red admiral butterflies. A solitary raven passed overhead, its familiar deep "krark" call echoing across the

Hemp agrimony at Golden.

valley. I wondered how many generations of the magnificent bird had passed this way, perhaps over thousands of years. And how many generations of humans had been in the valley to hear the raven?

There are remnants of the settlements of early people in the district. Behind us, on top of a tree-clad escarpment, stands one of their hill forts; an extensive area enclosed by a single bank and ditch. It is probably of Iron Age date, at least 2000 years old, once containing a community living in round huts made of timber, wattle and thatch. They were farmers, growing cereal crops and tending pigs and goats in small enclosed fields. They also utilised the riverside meadows, cutting a hay crop and herding cattle down the steep track to pasture on the moors, just as their successors do today. On the opposite side of the valley stands the Norman church of Creed, picturesque, with a splendid view towards the river. There is no sign of a nucleated settlement here; the parishioners were widely scattered, in the ancient farms that at intervals line the sides of the valley, and in the nearby planned town of Grampound.

Well over a thousand years went by from the time Golden fort was occupied until the founding of Creed church. But some of the parishioners who were laid to rest in the beautiful church-yard could have been from the same stock as those in the fort. There would have been little difference between them apart from the god, or gods, they worshipped. The language would have been basically the same, at least until gradual anglicization from the Later Middle Ages.

In the past people would have valued the river as a source of food; in the tidal reaches farming the beds of shellfish and erecting fish weirs to trap migrating eels and salmon. From the Middle Ages weirs were erected along the upper river to divert water to drive mills. Up until that time flour for bread making, a staple of life, was produced by grinding corn between quern stones, an arduous but necessary domestic activity. Apart from the technical construction of the buildings, Fal mills required careful surveying and digging of long leats parallel to the river, requiring negotiation and agreements with land owners. Some of these mills have disappeared, but the shells of others remain, as symbols of early industrial technology within a natural environment, subject to drought or flood.

A walker has to beware of the traffic at Tregony Bridge, as cars and vans are frequent at this "Gateway to the Roseland", only slowing down when passing each other between the narrow parapets of the bridge. It is an absolutely vital crossing point over the Fal Valley today. I wondered if its earliest predecessor, perhaps built of timber rather than stone, had been thought to be as essential when first built, said to have been in the year 1300 AD. It must have been commissioned by Lord Pomeroy, founder of the town of Tregony, whose little castle, on the hill above, guarded the crossing. The castle would have been clearly seen from across the valley, the Pomeroy family standard above the battlements fluttering in the breeze. I imagined the opening ceremony: the knight and his lady, escorted by a small retinue, progressing down the hill, cheered by grateful town and country folk. And the first horse-drawn wagon or string of pack mules crossing with local produce bound for Truro market, a day's march away.

I thought of the valley as a microcosm of Cornish history. So many people have lived, loved and died here over the ages. By their industry they have helped to form the valley as it is today. Did they think it beautiful – or did it just exist, as they did themselves? The lives and actions of the few of them recorded here must stand as tributes to those unknown people of the past, living beside the River Fal. What history will be written here over the next thousand years; will salmon still run in the river; will ravens still soar and call overhead; and will there be people here to notice them?

1. The Tinners of the Fal

The predominant rocks underlying much of the course of the Fal are sedimentary slates and sandstones of Devonian age, generally known locally as killas. These once lay as high ground over much of West Cornwall, until split apart and distorted by upthrusts of granite about 280 million years ago. The granites created the landscapes that typify Cornwall, that of Bodmin Moor, Carnmenellis, the Land's End, and, under the headwaters of the Fal, the St Austell granites. The tremendous forces involved in these earth movements brought about changes in the composition of adjacent rocks, introducing many mineral elements, particularly metal ores of tin and copper. Faults also weakened the underlying rock structure, some of which are said to have opened up to erosion and helped to create the Fal Valley and estuary of Carrick Roads.

During the last two million years of Ice Ages the Fal estuary and its tributaries were cut by a succession of inundations of meltwaters flowing southward from the heights of the spine of Cornwall, during spring thaws over a landscape that at times resembled the Arctic. The present diminutive River Fal was, at various times, a violent cataract, cutting deeply into the ancient rocks. The width and depth of the present valley, and other similar valleys egressing onto the Devon and Cornwall south coasts bear witness to the eroding power of fast flowing water, carrying its burden of rock debris towards the sea.

At the end of the last Ice Age, about twelve thousand years ago, as the polar ice caps melted, sea levels, which had been as low as 120 metres below the present height, were rapidly rising. The British Isles had once been connected by land bridge to Europe, the coast of Cornwall extending for miles further seawards than it does today. Now the rising waters were to break through to form the English Channel; the forests that had grown up on a Cornish coastal plain were gradually inundated. Sometimes today, at very low tides, the remnants of these forests may be seen in the sands. Samples of trees from the most well known, in Mount's Bay, have been dated to about 4300 years before present. The deep canyon that was to become Carrick Roads was slowly filled by the sea, to form a ria, backing up toward the tributaries that were now diminishing in their flow. But the evidence of their former power can be seen on the Fal in the deep narrow ravines at Retew, Crowhill, Lanihorne Woods and, of course, King Harry Reach.

Goss Moor, below the source of the Fal, lies over part of the St Austell granites, at an elevation of about 130 metres above sea level. The moor is rightly a national nature reserve, a "fascinating mosaic of wetland, heathland and scrub", as the guide book tells us. But it is also an example of the tenacity of nature over man's despoilation of the natural envi/onment. In comparatively recent times nature has been left to itself to reclothe a landscape once mined, dredged and streamed for tin and other minerals from the Bronze Age to the twentieth century.

Miners raising tin ore and carrying it to be crushed at the stamps mill, which is driven by an overshot water wheel. (Detail from a cartouche on Gascoyne's Map of Cornwall.)

In her *Tour through England on a side saddle* of 1695, that intrepid horsewoman Celia Fiennes gave a graphic description of mining to the west of St Austell. She saw the leats and timber launders taking water to overshot water-wheels, working to drain the excavations, the use of hand windlasses to raise buckets of ore from the shafts, and carried away to be crushed and smelted. She reckoned that twenty men and boys would work a mine, which was operated day and night. About one thousand were employed in that area. She had stayed in St Austell overnight, on her way to stay with her relation, Mr Boscawen, at Tregothnan, the magnificent mansion overlooking the Truro River. She does not give her route, but describes passing one hundred mines on the way, therefore she probably went via Polgooth and Sticker. Within 6 miles she arrives at – (the placename is left blank). This is obviously Tregony, for she passed over a long stone bridge (this is mainly causeway), and cut through the lanes to her destination.

Much of the flood plain of the Fal, on its short 18 mile course to the sea, has probably been prospected and "turned over" by the tinners in the past. They searched for the heavy dark pebbles of cassiterite, the tin ore, that had been torn from the metaliferous rocks upstream during Ice Age spates. It was carried down the valley with other rock debris, to lie deep within silty alluvial flood plain deposits. In the natural course of events a river will create a level flood plain, over many centuries cutting away and building up its banks, describing a snake-like meandering pattern that gradually moves down the valley. Tin streamers disrupted that pattern, as they washed the ores out of a matrix of sand and clay, using the power of flowing water from the river and artificial leats. Nature, the deposition of china clay waste, and perhaps farming practices, have since obscured these ancient workings.

Alluvial deposits would have naturally built up flood plain levels. Similarly, sand and mud banks are natural features of

A flood plain where tin streaming was once proposed. A view towards Tregony from Woodend. The river lies hidden on the right. Thorn scrub blocks the view towards the bridge. The river once meandered across the middle of this moor.

estuaries such as the Fal. However, from medieval times there were complaints that the washing of tin ores on the higher reaches of the rivers sent down so much debris that it clogged up the harbours. As early as 1356 the port of Lostwithiel was said to be threatened by waste sent down the Fowey River by tinners on Bodmin Moor. Later statutes to prevent the practice on the Fowey and Fal had little effect. The accumulation of mine and streaming waste was alleged by Hitchens in 1824, and copied by many others since, to be the reason why the supposed port of Tregony was deserted by the tide.

The practice of tin streaming is said to have begun to decline from the seventeenth century as deep mining techniques improved. However, as we shall see from the following local instances, it continued in some form or other into the twentieth century. During his *Travels through England* in 1750, Dr. Richard Pococke, while passing through Grampound, observed tin stream works on the east side of the Fal, presumably on the meadows below the bridge. Two sites, miles apart, are mentioned briefly by H. Michell Whitley in his discourse on the silting of the Fal in *Journal of the Royal Institution of Cornwall* volume 7, 1880: when discussing alluvial deposits he alludes to tin stream works at the Cornwall Railway viaduct in the Crowhill Valley. Another site had been half a mile below "Hayle Boat Rock", otherwise Halbote, not far above Tregony. Other observers have written about tin streaming close to the graveyard of St James church above Tregony Bridge. In a dual monograph deposited in the Cornwall Record Office, a Tregony resident wrote that shortly after 1849 he saw miners searching for tin ore on the church site. A considerable quantity of cassiterite pebbles were found. He added that an old man had told him that his father remembered tin streamers on the same site playing bowls with about 150 skulls they had unearthed.[1]

Other works were carried out, or at least permission was given, on sites on the flood plain below Tregony Bridge, down as far as the tidal limit: in 1747 an agreement was made between land owner Francis Gregor of Trewarthenick and tinners Alexander Bono and Peter Toago to lease the Hopeful Tin Bounds in the parish of Cornelly (the west side of the river, which formed the parish boundary); the bounds are described in detail. Another example dates from 1804: Francis Gregor, presumably the son of the former, gave authority to John Williams of Scorrier (a very big name in mining circles) to:

> "dig work stream and search for tin and tin ores over the unimproved Moores of Trelasker and Trewarthenick in the Parish of Cornelly, on the west side of the River Fal running from Tregony Bridge southward ... commonly called by the name of Salmon House ... also (to) Ruan Lanihorne ... Commonly called Sea (?) Moore ... extending as far south as with the Glebe lands of Ruan Lanihorne ... the Alder Moor, the Long Moor, Lower Trelask Moor, Higher Trelask Moor ... and all the watercourses through ... for the better working and streaming ..."[2]

The agreement was for 21 years. The ground was to be restored at the finish of the work, under a penalty of £5. Gregor is believed to have received shares in any profits. Hopefully some provision was made for the working of Nansaker Mill which stood in the middle of the proposed area. It is not known if part or any of the above work was actually carried out.

The same applies to another project that had been proposed for the area some years previously, although not actually associated with tin streaming. During the years 1775-7 there was correspondence between Francis Gregor and Lord Falmouth at Tregothnan, the extensive adjoining estate down the valley. Gregor suggested that a canal might be cut to straighten the river where the meanders were particularly sinuous, thereby improving an area of "rushy grounds" on the flood plain. The area was roughly between the house called Porters and Lanihorne Wood. A detailed plan of the proposed changes was sent. The river was the boundary between Gregor's Trelasker Moor and, on the east side, Trethewye Moor in the Barton of Trethewye, then held by Lord Falmouth. The small pieces of ground would be swopped. The narrow turnpike road from Tregony to Ruan runs close to the river at this point. Gregor would take on the cost and seek tenders for the work. He received the following letter, sent from "Falmouth House" on 20 January 1776:

"Sir ... I have already assured you I am willing to oblige you provided I can be assured the changing the bed and course of the river will not be prejudicial to my Royalty thereof (his fishery rights etc), you allow it is right and necessary to be certain that will be secure to me unimpeached, as this is not the time of year for business of this kind, consideration of my right will not delay it.

Lady Falmouth, Mr. Boscowen and self beg to return our sincere compliments to all the family at Trewarthenick wishing them many happy years.

I am Sir, your sincere friend and servant, Falmouth".

Gregor's letter had been delayed – "by the impediment of the Post occasioned by a great fall of snow which rendered the roads impassable several days."

A further plan, with seals attached, in the Gregor archives, dated 18 June 1777, indicates that the agreement was confirmed.[3] Later tin streaming may have masked any signs of the completion of a canal. It is plain that Gregor's scheme was to improve the "rushy grounds". There is no indication that he wished to alleviate any flooding problems or build up of alluvial deposits, but to create useable pasture. Sheep happily graze there today, albeit on a grass carpet with underlay of china clay waste.

2. Mills of the Clay Country

For centuries the waters of the Fal and its tributaries have been harnessed to power mills. In the comparatively wet Cornish climate, generally those streams, draining from the rocks of the surrounding hills, have a reliable flow. However, with a comparatively short distance to run before reaching the sea, they did not have the volume to drive big undershot water-wheels. Therefore, in common with most of the wheels powering the mining district, the overshot system was generally used. Water was delivered via a leat to the top of the wheel, turning it by the weight of water in the buckets or shrouds, which filled and emptied as the wheel turned. The leat was an artificial ditch or channel beginning at a dam or "head weir" on the river at a distance upstream of the mill. The distance depended on the gradient of the river from that point giving a

Cartoon of an early overshsot water-mill, depicting a wooden launder to the top of the wheel.

sufficient "head" of water to the wheel. On the Fal the leats ran more or less parallel to the river, following the contours on the edge of the flood plain. The flow of water from the leat was delivered to the top of the wheel usually via a launder or wooden channel. The mill building itself was usually on the edge of the flood plain, raised above flood levels. Mills were leased by the owner of the land, perhaps the Lord of the Manor, who obtained revenue from them. Leases incorporated rights to take water from the river and control of head weir sluices and leats.

On the Fal, and a few of its tributaries, the waters mainly powered corn or grist mills, grinding cereals into flour for bread making or use as animal feed; they were vital to the local community. Water power was also used for industrial purposes: it seems that even very small mills were capable of driving hammers for beating or "fulling" material in cloth production. During the last three centuries the infant Fal, not far from its source, was also made to work for other and perhaps even more important purposes.

The headwaters of the Fal rise in the high ground to the north and west of St Austell. The area, sometimes known as Hensborough, was once similar in appearance to much of West Cornwall: there was some moorland, but otherwise it was a landscape of stone-walled fields and scattered farmsteads, some of which could have had their foundations in the Bronze or Iron Age. Few people, apart from those prospecting for tin, copper or iron, could suspect that beneath their feet there lay vast deposits of a special type of granite. Over millions of years it had decomposed into what we know today as kaolin or china clay. William Cookworthy's discovery of the clay in the mid-eighteenth century was to lead to its use in a great variety of products now thought essential to modern life. Initially the main use was in the making of pottery, companies such as Wedgwood leasing one or more setts or mining claims. Today it is said that about eighty per cent is used in the paper-making industry; much of it is exported for this use. By the mid-nineteenth century annual clay production figures had reached 65,000 tons, and continued to rise. The many small mining companies were eventually replaced by a single body; working methods and conditions improved. In the twentieth century annual production figures reached over two million tons. China clay became one of the Country's most successful exports.

The clay's extraction by open-cast mining has led to the devastation of about 24 square miles of ancient countryside. The huge white sky tips, or "Cornish Alps", of excavated waste material, consisting of overburden, quartz, sand and mica, can be seen from afar, although some have now been landscaped and seeded to resemble a more natural form. Some of the phenomenally deep pits are still worked; others, with their attendant mica dams, refineries and railway lines, left to nature. Many millions of tons of rock have been taken from the earth, each ton of productive rock processed resulted in the average extraction of just fifteen per cent of china clay.

In the early years material for export was taken to the nearest shipment port by packhorse teams or horse-drawn wagons. In the 1840s the great innovating entrepreneur Joseph Treffry built a tramway from St Dennis, situated on the northern side of the clay mining area, to the new port of Newquay on the north coast. This allowed goods such as coal from South Wales to be brought in and cargoes of china clay, china stone and other products taken out. The clay and stone were perhaps sailed up to the River Mersey, en route to The Potteries via canal transport. Horse-drawn trucks were used on the tramway, cables on an incline plane being used to drag the trucks back up out of Newquay onto higher ground. On 1 May 1857 the *West Briton* newspaper reported that the line had been opened to passenger traffic. A large number of people assembled at St Dennis, to be taken on flag-bedecked carriages

The River Fal flows under Trerice Bridge, deep in the wooded valley below Wheel Remfry china clay tip.

Buddleia colonising the multi-coloured waste granite on Wheal Remfry tip.

to Newquay. The carriages, two of which carried china stone for export, were each drawn by a single horse. On long portions of track with a shallow descent the horses were unhitched and the carriages went on their way " ... at almost locomotive speed."

During the next few decades other lines were built in the clay area, being incorporated into the Cornwall Minerals Railway. Steam locomotives were used from 1869 and connections made with the Main Line. The main china clay export ports were to comprise Fowey, Par, Charlestown and Pentewan. Some clay was exported from the new Falmouth Docks after the opening of the Falmouth Branch Line in 1863. Today only Fowey operates as a commercial port for the clay; ships are often seen at the loading wharves above the town.

China stone, a feldspar and fluorspar-rich, much harder and more friable rock than china clay, was mined from the mid-nineteenth century until about 1965, mainly from quarries in the St Stephen in Brannel area. Being less contaminated than the clay, it was used as a flux and in slips and glazes in the production of high quality ceramics. When mined, it was broken into fist-sized lumps and taken to grinding mills as part of the refining process. In the early years some stone was shipped direct to potters such as Wedgwood who had their own mills. A number were also built on a Fal tributary close to the quarries in the Tregargus Valley to the north of St Stephen.

A grinding mill was a massive stone-built structure containing two or more circular tanks or pans built of brick or stone. Each had revolving grinding mechanisms driven from central gearing between the tanks. These in turn were powered by a large iron-built overshot water-wheel. The process to grind the stone into an ultra-fine slurry could take up to twenty-four hours. It was then run off for refining processes and to settling pans or drys, here, with the assistance of underfloor heating from a furnace,

The derelict Trevear China Stone Mill, Tregargus Valley, St Stephen.

it settled to a certain consistency. It was then cut into blocks for transportation. That is a very basic explanation of a complicated and highly skilled operation. The refining of china clay and china stone could result in a great number of different grades; in modern works computers assist in the refining process. The remains of a number of china stone mills exist in the Tregargus Valley. Water to drive them came via a number of leats from the headwaters of the small stream, known here as the Barn River, that runs southwards, past the village of Coombe, to join the Fal at Trenowth Bridge, Crowhill. At least two of these mills were also situated on the main River Fal.

Goss Moor lies at a height of about 130 metres above sea level. From there the land falls away southwards through China Clay Country. Within 5 miles, at the village of St Stephen, the elevation has dropped to 72 metres. The River Fal becomes a considerable stream as it follows suit. Over the millennia it has cut a deep winding valley through soft rock, on its way passing through the Retew Gorge. This takes its name from the old village of Retew, which in the 1960s was abandoned and lost under the vast clay works of Wheal Remfry. It is believed to be one of six villages and hamlets in the area removed by the clay companies so that they could extract the clay from beneath them. The Wheal Remfry pit, perhaps up to 100 metres in depth, with its attendant refinery, settling tanks and drys, extends for about a mile, its waste tips looming above the west bank of the Fal. Looking across the vale of the Fal from an easterly location near Roche, the Wheal Remfry tip stands out as a gigantic white scar covering the high ground to the west. Further southwards, the original Virginia and Melbur Works lie as one vast excavation for almost 2 miles to Terras, close to St Stephen.

The now abandoned Retew Branch of the Cornwall Minerals Railway lay between the river and the clay works. Little of its course is now visible here; parts of the valley have been taken over by natural regeneration of tree growth, particularly sycamore. At Melbur there were sidings and loading facitilies for the products from the adjacent works. This location was known as Melbur Mill, and sometimes Meledor Mill; the former name may be a corruption of the latter. A long leat, also on the western bank of the Fal, once provided water to the refinery and, originally to Meledor corn mill.

Begun in the 1820s, the clay works gradually took over Meledor village and agricultural land that was once part of the ancient Meledor Manor. The sixteenth century farmhouse and nearby great stone barn still stand forlornly on private land within the confines of Melbur refinery. The two-storeyed house is constructed of granite rubble and cob. It was listed Grade II in 1952, although it had been considerably altered over the years. It was still occupied in the 1980s but has since become inaccessible because of trees and undergrowth. The Manor corn mill, the first from the river's source, is now assumed to be lost, but certainly existed until the beginning of the twentieth century. According to *Kelly's Directory*, Henry Truscott was miller there in 1873. He was still there, as miller and cow keeper, in 1889. A gravestone in Creed churchyard is dedicated to William Pomery Arthur, who died in 1917, and Emily his wife, 1905; the couple had lived at Meledor Mill.

The river meanders down from Melbur for nearly a mile before passing under the road bridge at Terras, just to the west of St Stephen. It was accompanied by another leat, from Melbur, on its western side, which passed under the road into Terras China Stone Mill. This is believed to have operated from the 1890s until about 1930. Its appearance and operation was similar to those at Tregargus, as described above. It is said to have had an iron overshot wheel with the impressive dimensions of 28 feet in diameter and 7 feet in width. Remnants of the mill lie on private land close to the road. The wheel has gone, but some of the stone-built features lie deep beneath a thicket of wild scrub and brambles. However, the floor of the great Dry, where the refined clay slurry was dried by underfloor heating, still exists; it is now used for storage. Remarkably, it is still covered by what is believed to be the original, although frequently repaired, corrugated iron roof. Its remarkable rusted red colour is striking enough to draw local artists to paint it.

Southwards from Terras, the river is generally enclosed within a sylvan ribbon snaking across the flood plain meadows. A single-track road, deepened by centuries of travellers, follows in the same direction. However, it cannot keep close to the river, but has to take a course along the valley sides over a terrain which is decidedly lumpy. It sometimes runs over high ground where distant views of the river in its deep valley may be seen, before suddenly plunging and twisting in and out of tributary-cut side valleys., often beneath a high canopy of oak trees. Within less than a mile it reaches the hamlet of Trelyon and passes over the Fal to arrive at Tolgarrick Farm and its adjacent mill.

Tolgarrick Corn Mill, the second from the source, is featured on the 1813 Ordnance Survey Map. At that time the area was

The great barn at Meledor Farm, constructed of granite rubble.

The impressive roof of the clay-drying building at Terras.

owned by John Trevanion Bettesworth Trevanion of Caerhays, the well-known estate on the coast of the Roseland. In April 1829 he assigned the tenure of the mill at Tolgarrick to a Robert Dyer. It included about 12 acres of land; the whole was previously in the Tenure of Thomas Cock.[4] In December 1860 John Dyer (presumably Robert Dyer's son), flour dealer of St Austell, and Jane Rogers of St Ewe, spinster, granted a seven year lease to Patrick Cruickshank and John Dickenson Brenton, both of London. The lease gave them rights over – "All that stream of water running through the farm and lands of Tolgarrick … except so much water as will be sufficient to work the flour or grist mill upon the said farm … and also full liberty to cut any leat or head weir … to convey the said stream in such manner the grantees think fit."

This must refer to the mill leat that left the river at some distance upstream, rather than the river itself. The grantees were to make and repair the hatches (sluice gates) at their expense. Also keep and repair the banks of the channel and the launder to the mill wheel behind the house and premises, part of the farm occupied by John Hooper Rouse.[5] The purpose of that "stream of water" was probably to supply a newly-established iron ore treatment works, situated between the mill and the river. At about this time, a mine, South Terras, was opened up to the south of Tolgarrick Farm, with shafts and adits close by. Initially it was to exploit an iron ore lode, however, in about 1889, at a depth of about 40 fathoms, a new company reached high grade deposits of pitchblend. South Terras was **to** become "the most famous uranium mine in Britain." The lode was followed for a considerable distance, including under the Fal. Over 700 tons of highly radioactive ore was eventually extracted. A refinery works was established on the iron ore site by the river. It included a waterwheel driving flat rods to a set of ore stamps. A tall chimney for a furnace was also built.

Above: At Tolgarrick. *Below:* Tolgarrick Mill.

The true value of uranium, commercially and to humankind, was not known at the time; it was only used for such purposes as colouring in glass production. It was not until 1904 that Marie Curie, using ore samples from European mines, isolated radium. In 1912 the mine was bought by a French company, but it eventually folded after a series of disputes with the landlords, by this time the Boconnoc Estate. Another company attempted to re-open it in 1928 but also failed. It was abandoned in 1930. It is not known how much valuable ore remains to be discovered, nor how many miners received lethal doses of radiation as they worked, fell sick and died, not knowing the cause.

The little stone-built mill stands close to the farmhouse. It is tucked into the side of the wooded hill, and is in a very dilapi- dated state; it is bereft of wheel and machinery and at present (2016) the slate roof needs urgent attention. Access to view the leat is not possible. The lack of a substantial population in the area leads one to suppose that the mill generally ground animal feed rather than high-grade flour. A grove of trees and scrub stands between the farmhouse and the river. Within it lie the bases of buildings and chimney of the abandoned iron ore and uranium processing works. Surface areas are believed to be still radioactive.

Less than a mile downstream the river drops out of sight into the beautiful and secret Crowhill Valley, a Site of Special Scien- tific Interest. Within the valley a head weir let water into an artificial leat which ran down through the ancient Trenowth Wood. At the bottom of the valley, on the Ladock road, and almost beneath the great viaduct of the Cornwall Railway, stands Trenowth Mill. The site is ancient, and we must admire the people who originally carved a leat through that rocky terrain to supply water to the wheel. The leat still forms part of the Parish or District Boundary.

Spring cow parsley ("Queen Anne's Lace") on a local lane.

In May 1333 Michael deTrenowth, of Pydar Hundred, found himself liable for certain debts, having to declare to the Chancery the values of property he held. He gave evidence that he owned certain land and tenements in Trenowth, including a water-mill.[6] In March the following year Michael again had to declare his assets. These included a corn mill, presumably the same as the previous year, and also a fulling mill, probably working off the same leat.[7] For the next few hundred years the record appears to be blank. It is not until 1806 that we find a mill still occupies the site. In February a letter between John Groggin and Sir C. Hawkins (presumably Christopher Hawkins of Trewithen), discussing other business, mentions that Trenowth Mill needs a new wheel. The following year Hawkins took out a mortgage on one sixth of the value of the mill.

The present building couldn't be more different from the little Tolgarrick Mill further upstream: it is an imposing four storeys in height on a rectangular plan; built of local shale rubble with granite and brick dressings. The original building may have

The imposing
Trenowth Mill.

been just two storeys in height; changes in the original stonework indicate that the extra storeys were added to it, possibly in the eighteenth century. It is not known when the mill ceased working. Since then it has been sympathetically restored and is now a private residence, as is the adjacent attractive Miller's House. The mill's original jettied loading door on the front of the top floor has been replaced by an attic window. No wheel or machinery survives, but the leat can be traced, running along the side of the hill towards the back of the mill. The building has been given Grade II listing. Listing information states that a stone on the west end of the ground floor is inscribed *M. Brewer 1896*. There may be a family connection with the miller named Brewer who was at Golden Mill in 1828. The 1880 O.S. Map of Trenowth clearly shows the leat going to the back of the building. It must have been at a high enough level for the timber launder to take water to an overshot wheel on the western side. Infilling of the stonework indicates that the wheel axle was once there. The tail race went under the road and across the fields below.

The 1907 O.S. Map depicts significant changes: a small building had been built close to the leat to the east of the

Crowhill Railway Viaduct lies beyond the Trenowth Bridge over the Fal.

Miller's House. This must have contained the small iron-built water-wheel, remains of which still exist. Its function is unknown. The leat had also been extended for about one hundred yards beyond the mill, where it passed through a large stone culvert under the road into Trenowth China Stone Mill. Here, as at Tregargus and Terras, there were water-driven grinding mills and associated works. It is not known why this isolated rural spot was chosen for such an industrial purpose, apart from a good flow of water from the leat. Presumably the raw china stone was brought down from St Stephen by horse-drawn, or possibly steam, wagon, fortunately mostly downhill. The finished product could have been taken to nearby Grampound Road Station for rail transportation to the docks. Going by the example of Terras, the mill may have closed in about 1930. There are no visible remains on the site, the building materials removed and possibly used elsewhere.

The flood plain and viaduct over the Crowhill Valley.

Grampound

Grampound Bridge over the "White River" in the early twentieth century. (Royal Institution of Cornwall.)

The small town of Grampound, some might term it a village, clings to a steep slope on the eastern side of the Fal Valley. The properties line each side of the busy A390 road where it plunges down to the valley bottom and passes over the river. It was a planned town, with burgage plots set out on either side of the road, founded in about 1296 by John, Earl of Cornwall. The possible intention was to provide services for his nearby manor of Tybesta. It lies on the edge of the parish of Creed, where a mile away the little parish church is beautifully situated overlooking the valley. The modern civil parish is designated Grampound with Creed.

Under a charter of 1332 the vill was given the status of a Free Borough, with gild merchants, two fairs and a market. The burgesses were given Tybesta corn and fulling mills, situated at the bottom of the town. The Hundred of Powder Court was to be held here on a regular basis. The survey of the Duchy of

Above:
Grampound,
looking east
along Fore
Street.

Right:
Grampound
Town Hall and
Clock Tower on
Fore Street.

Cornwall property in 1337 stated that in "Grauntpont" there were 28 burgages. There were 40 acres of land and about 60 acres of waste. The pattern of medieval strip fields, surrounded by later enclosures, lies alongside the main road to the east of the town. A chapel dedicated to St Mary was built in the town in about 1400. However, the population were probably expected to walk a mile to worship at Creed church.

The narrow Creed road runs southwards along the eastern flank of the valley to the church before rising up onto higher ground towards Tregony and the Roseland. Its beginning at Grampound is not easy to spot, being a narrow entrance halfway along Fore Street. Almost opposite, close to the Town Clock, another narrow entrance takes the explorer northwards along a tortuous lane towards Coombe and St Stephen. These two minor highways may be of great age, forming a continuous route north and south along the side of the Fal Valley.

The town is situated on the ancient southern main highway into West Cornwall, where, after following a route over comparatively level ground to the east and west, the deep valley of the Fal had to be negotiated. The town's name is derived from the French for great bridge, although the first simple bridges must pre-date the foundation of the place. In 1308 it was referred to as Ponsmur, apparently the equivalent term in the Cornish language.

It has been suggested that the Romans built a bridge here. This is unlikely, as the Roman presence in West Cornwall seems to have been practically non-existent, at least from the second century AD. In later centuries a simple timber bridge may have been sufficient for horses and pack animals to pass over the comparatively small river, except perhaps when it was in spate. Presumably the cost of a stone bridge was funded at the foundation of the town, and called "great bridge" because there was only a simple structure there before. The width of the arches of the medieval bridge would have been limited by the existing construction techniques and available materials; apparently in 1750 the bridge had five arches. That number may have been thought necessary to span the width of the valley and allow for flood relief. That bridge was demolished in 1834. A two arched bridge replaced it, which in turn was superseded in 1968 by a concrete structure strong enough to cope with modern heavy traffic.

The town, more or less equidistant between Truro and St Austell, was too close to either to gain much benefit as a rest point for travellers passing along this major western highway. In the sixteenth century John Norden described it as: "Of small resorte, the town very ancient, the priviledge (as a Borough) large but the inhabitants few and poor." Richard Carew, in his Survey of 1602, was also not very impressed:

"Grampond, if it took that name from any great bridge, hath now *nomen sine re* (the name without the thing) for the bridge here is supported with only a few arches, and the corporation but half replenished with inhabitants, who may better vaunt their town's antiquity than the town of their ability."

Norden's and Carew's remarks allude to the town being a "pocket borough", one of 20 pocket or rotten boroughs in Cornwall, each electing two members to Parliament. They were part of a corrupt English electoral system which lasted for centuries. The Lord of the Manor or chief landowner usually owned most of the tenements occupied by the few householders eligible to vote. Therefore they could be "persuaded", or otherwise bribed, to vote for his chosen candidates. (Grampound didn't send two members to Parliament until 1547.) In 1800 there were 85 houses with about 200 inhabitants in the town, of which only 25 were eligible to vote. The place was said to be notorious for corruption. At one election the Freemen had been known to boast of receiving 300

Grampound
Corn Mill, one of
several buildings
in the industrial
complex.

guineas each for their vote. Probably as a consequence, Grampound was disenfranchised in 1821, eleven years before the Reform Act which deprived other places, including St. Mawes and Tregony, of their doubtful privileges.

Apart from such excitements the general population would have carried on with their lives as farmhands, workers in various trades, and shopkeepers. The town was well known for its tanneries, which operated until recent times. In the seventeenth century it was said: "The inhabitants here drive a considerable trade for gloves here made."

At the end of Mill Lane, close to the river, stand the impressive buildings of Grampound water-mills. They probably lie over the site of the medieval Tybesta Manor mills. The Duchy survey of 1337 stated that the burgesses held two corn mills, one being a "new" mill, and a fulling mill, rendering yearly 10 marks. (According to Halliday the annual rent for the manorial mills was 53 shillings and 4 pence.) Three hundred years later the burgesses still controlled the rents, issuing leases for the town corn mills in 1677, and the fulling mills at various times in the seventeenth century.[8] (Although Benny states that "it is recorded" that in June 1607 Grampound mills were sold by Francis Tregian to Ezechiell Grose.)

A succession of buildings have stood on this ancient site, being enlarged and adapted over the years, depending on their industrial uses. The leat, about a mile in length, provided enough water to power three wheels. It began at a head weir on the river in the vicinity of Trevan Wood and followed the contours on the eastern side, parallel to the river, down to the mills. At the beginning of the nineteenth century a woollen mill was being operated by Thomas Seccombe; on 19 November 1813 the following advertisement appeared in the *West Briton* newspaper:

"Grampound Yarn Manufactury

A person who well understands the management of carding and scribbling engines, billies, jannies, etc., is wanted at the above manufactory as a foreman, and if of a religious character the more acceptable. Apply to Thomas Seccombe, Grampound."

On 23 June 1820 a further advertisement from Seccombe appeared in the same newspaper. This time he advertised the lease of a newly erected fulling mill, called Grampound Spinning Mill, giving details of the machinery for making woollen yarn; a constant stream of water was assured. This mill continued to work into the twentieth century for various industrial purposes including a glove manufactory. The corn mill, by then using electricity to augment water power, did not close until 1974. At the end of quiet Mill Lane, the several buildings are an impressive sight. It is hoped that some restoration will take place to preserve them for the future: they are a major part of the history of Grampound.

The growth of industry, particularly mining, and later tourism, brought a few opportunities for the population to benefit from increasing traffic on the main arterial highway passing their front doors, especially after 1821 when it became a turnpike road. An 1830 directory describes the town as having three inns and a number of shopkeepers and tradesmen and women. The list includes a grocer and two butchers, drapers, tailor, dressmaker and shoemaker. Other tradesmen included two carpenters and builders, blacksmith, stonemason, nurseryman and three maltsters. Also listed were three tanners and three curriers working in the well-known Grampound tanneries. The Truro to St Austell carriers passed through the town daily. A century later *Kelly's Directory* was listing a very similar number of shop keepers and artisans, now with modern additions such as a motor garage and cycle agent.

Although traditional local shops and other services have been lost over the years, down by the bridge there is a thriving village hall and a community owned shop. Much of the village is a Conservation Area, with about 20 listed buildings lining Fore Street, including the dominant Town Hall and Clock Tower. Not forgetting the preserved Manor Tannery and Town Mills, formerly employers of generations of the local population.

Footbridge across the Fal at Golden Moor, below Grampound.

4. Golden Mill

Further down the Fal Valley the hills still press in on either side, with the apparent intention of coming together to regain their territory lost during the Ice Ages. A mile or so down on the west bank, overlooking the unfrequented Golden Bridge, there stand the ramparts of one of the largest "hill forts" in Cornwall. Although unexcavated, it is likely to be of an early Iron Age date. It is now surrounded by trees but its commanding position above the Fal may be judged from the map: although there is level ground to the west, the other sides are defended by steep ravines to the north and south and by the Fal river. Close to the bridge stands lonely Golden Mill. It is accessed from the west via a sunken minor road, passing the

The two Golden Mill buildings, tucked below the tree-covered ramparts of the Iron Age hill fort.

A discarded "coge wheel", possibly a pit wheel, at Golden. A few wooden teeth remain in situ.

historic Golden Manor House and an ancient chapel in a farmyard. Golden, the medieval Wolveden, is well-known because of the 1577 attack on the house and arrest of the owner, the Elizabethan recusant Francis Tregian, who was harbouring a Catholic priest. After a trial at Launceston the priest was executed. Tregian's wife and family were thrown out of the house and he lost the estates, spending many years in the Fleet Prison.

At the bottom of the hill, the handsome stone two-storeyed mill buildings and barn form a group partly surrounding a courtyard. The site is privately owned, deserted at the time of writing. There are no signs of water-wheels, or where the leats or launders reached the mill, nor the tail race. However, these can be deduced from the early large-scale Ordnance Survey maps. In the Cornwall Record Office there is a very rough sketch map depicting the mill leat. The map is undated but, from the style of writing, could be eighteenth century or earlier. The leat is shown leaving the Fal via a head weir, on the west side of the Fal, a little way upstream of Grampound Bridge, passing southwards under the A390 road. Apart from the first

200 yards or so, the leat's course downstream cannot be easily accessed, but can be seen on the early map, following the contours through woodland to the mill.

The history of the mill site is said to go back to the time of Henry VIII, when a John Trevanyon (of Caerhays?) leased Golden tenement. He lodged a bond of one hundred pounds to have a head weir built to raise water levels on the Fal to improve the operation of Golden Mill. In 1637 articles of agreement were made at Golden, between Ezechiell Grose and carpenter Thomas Toprell of Creed. Grose had been miller at Grampound in 1607 and was obviously still in possession thirty years later, having rights over the riverside lands of Grampound Common and Penberthowe Moor, situated upstream of the bridge. Toprell was contracted to build a new head weir for Golden Mills leat, spanning the river below Grampound Mills. The objective was to provide enough water for *both mills* at Golden, probably meaning two wheels, to grind together. This implies that Grose was also leasing Golden Mills.[9] Repairs to the mill were being carried out in 1716. The leat is mentioned in a document of 1747 delineating the tin bounds in the Carvossa area.

By about 1800 the mill may have been out of use, or at least in a bad state of repair. It was then that millwright James Yeoman of Probus was asked to send in an estimate for major work to be done.[10] The estimate reveals that there were two overshot water-wheels, each driving separate sets of machinery to one, or perhaps two, sets of stones. It is not clear if the wheels were both on one building or two, as a section of the estimate is headed "The Uprite Mill". However, two buildings now exist.

Most items had to be custom made, or perhaps reconditioned, by the millwright. They included two new wooden wheels, 11 feet in diameter by 2 feet 6 inches wide (cost £22.10s.each);

Above: Spring
ramsons at
Golden.

Left:
Hartstongue
and male ferns
clothe the
shaded banks of
the byeways.

Creed church. In the spring the graveyard is covered with primroses.

Gravelly banks below Golden.

one axletree, 11 feet long by 17 inches diameter (£12.10s). A "mane coge wheel", possibly the pit wheel, 6 feet 9 inches in diameter (£13.10s.). Another "coge wheel", of 7 feet diameter (£14.14s). Iron items, that had to be cast, included the stone nut and main spur wheel. Many other items are listed but not easily interpreted. The estimate for one mill was £103.1s., and for the "Upright Mill", £81.7s.

In 1822 a bill and receipt were issued for the construction of the barn (presumably the present one) at Golden Mill.[11] In 1828 there was an estate assessment of the value of the mill tenement, including a barn, drainage to improve the land, and so on, making the whole, occupied by the miller Brewer £95, possibly the annual rent. The most interesting and unusual detail about the assessment is that it included a threshing machine driven by one of the mill wheels, possibly through some sort of belt drive arrangement.[12] Nothing relating to the later history of the mill has been found.

The Golden Mill group consists of the long barn, two presumed mill buildings, and adjacent miller's house. All are believed to be listed Grade II. They are estimated to have been built around 1800, or at least substantially refurbished from earlier buildings on the site. It is not known why the Bullers, the Golden Estate owners, decided to make such a large financial outlay at this time. Perhaps, seeing no end to the war with Napoleon, they envisaged long-term problems with food imports, and decided to concentrate on cereal production on the estate farms.

All the buildings were constructed using the local slatey "killas" rock. The two mill buildings have granite quoins. They are slightly different in construction, and one slightly larger than the other. They sit side by side, set into the side of the steep slope behind them, so that the leat, running along the side of the hill from Grampound, delivered the water to the back of

River meander above Tregony, adopting the natural inclination to cut into the bend's outer bank, in spite of attempts at protection.

the buildings at about second floor level; in other words, to the top of the 11 foot diameter water-wheels. Presumably, of the two wheels in Yeoman's estimate (above), each one was situated on the side of a building, with similar stones and machinery inside; timber launders took water from the leat to the wheels.

The larger building appears to be in excellent condition; the other is dilapidated, with a temporary roof replacing the, presumably hipped, original one. The buildings appear to be devoid of machinery, apart from a cast iron "coge wheel", possibly a pit wheel, still with a few wooden cogs in place, leaning against an outside wall.

5. Tregony Mill

One of the earliest records concerning this mill comes from *The Caption of Seisin* of 1337; the survey and valuation of property within the newly created Duchy of Cornwall. Apart from the few lands held by Henry de la Pomeroy, the only other Tregony asset listed is "One weak water mill (*molendinam aquaticum)* which used to render 30 shillings". This was probably a corn mill rather than a fulling mill, the latter being less common in Cornwall at this date. It is likely to have been near the same site as the later Pomeroy or Tregony town mill.

The early mill seems to have suffered from the work of tin streamers, or perhaps just a natural build-up of alluvium: Charles Henderson, in his *Ecclesiastical History*, wrote that in 1585 "John Rawe, Vicar of St James and Kybye (Cuby), exhibited a bill in the Exchequer against Hugh Pomeroy esq. for building a mill on part of the glebe known as 'Vycars Alders in the Vycars Moor.'" He alleged that fifty years previously John Trevanyon Esq. had a lease of Pomeroy's mills which, becoming overwhelmed with gravel, he procured Sir Edward Mann, then vicar, to allow him to erect a new mill on the vicar's land. In a document of 1602 on "The Present state of the vicaridge of James and Cuby" it is stated that "There belongeth a certain gryst mill unto the said vicaridge".[13] The mill was still owned by the Church in 1680, when its watercourse, leat, and "a lane leading to Tregony Mill" are given as boundaries to properties listed in a terrier describing the church glebe. Mill Lane still exists, dropping steeply down from the top of the Tregony Hill road to the river meadow below. On 1 September 1726 Henry Phillips, mill keeper, obtained a lease of Tregony Mill from Hugh, Viscount Falmouth. At the same time he also obtained a lease of "Yeoman's House" in Tregony.[14] This means therefore, that Boscawen, Lord Falmouth, had become owner of the mill at some time after 1680.

In *Pigot's Directory* of 1830 Nicholas Courtney is listed as miller at Tregony. On 7 August 1838 he advertised in the *West Briton* that the mills were to be let by tender: consisting of two treble mills, with a full stream of water in the driest summer, with outhouses and gardens, an acre of coarse ground and two very rich meadows. He stated that the mills were in good corn country and that, rather ambitiously, business could be extended towards St Mawes, Mevagissey, St Austell and Truro. John Brewer took up the lease, and is listed as miller in *Robinson's Commercial Directory* of 1840. Could he be the miller named Brewer who was at Golden Mill in 1828?

Cheap imported grain and modern milling methods, were to help towards the mill's closure, although no final date is known. Knowing its long history of providing bread for the community, it is strange to stand on the ancient mill platform above the marshy meadow and wonder how such a mill could so completely disappear. It is regrettable that no known illustrations were made of it before its demise. We are left with a few traces of the leat near where it left the river at Golden, and a unique document recording the apparent lack of proper management of the leat by an early tenant of the mill, described below.

Among the Golden estate archives in the Cornwall Record Office there is a deposition apparently written by, or for, the unnamed plaintiff (written Ptfs in the text), at an estimated date of circa 1700. It concerns the case of a complaint regarding the flooding of Golden Moors, the meadows above and below Golden Bridge, by the tenant of Tregony Mills (possibly damaging a hay crop?). The text informs us that Golden

Moors are the inheritance of Mr Buller (of Golden Manor), the plaintiff probably being his tenant. Lord Falmouth (Boscawen) is the owner of Tregony Mills, "let at a rack rent to the defendant Kittoo". However, the text states that the mills were the Bests' Mills, the Bests being the perpetrators of the flooding. The following edited text of the document demonstrates what could be involved in providing water to a mill wheel, in the context of the history of the Fal Valley. Particularly, the area called Halbote, now identified as being close to Golden Bridge.

"... an ancient watercourse runs from the said river into a mill leate in a close called Halbort and from the said close into and through that parte of Golden Moore which lyeth in Cuby which is on the east side of the said river and from thence to the Bests Mill called Tregony Mills. Sometimes in summertime that watercourse ... is not sufficient to drive the wheels of Tregony Mills so that Antiently an headweare (weir) was erected athwart the said river to turn an additional stream into an antient trench in that parte of Golden Moore ... and from thence into that antient leat there ... so ye same may run from thence unto Tregony Mills. The use of that antient head weare ... hath been discontinued for above 35 years last past and quite washed away.

Tregony and St James' Moor from the site of Tregony Mill.

Mr Trevanion having gotten an Act of Parliament to make the River Fala navigable did at least 15 or 20 years ago erect a sluice in the said river about fifty foot to the south of the said antient headweare with stones and earth. About 7 years since Tregony mills wanting water in the summer time one Warmington who was then tenant of the said mills erected an headweare … in or near the place where the said sluice beforehand stood which was then … washed away.

The said Mr Trevanion fayling in his undertaking and the said Warmington by means of his new erected headweare turned some of the water of the said river into the trench in Golden Moor in Cuby that the same might run into the antient leat there and from there to Tregony Mills … When the occupants of Tregony Mills made use of the … headweare to turn some part of the water of the said river into the trench in Golden Moore … (they) always took care that the water so turned into the said trench might not overflow the said moore but that redundancy of water … should be carried through another trench … back into the said river.

So that if the Bests had re-erected their headweare … where the same antiently stood and had prevented the water from overflowing the said moore this action would be spared. But the Bests instead of repairing ye antient headweare have made a new headweare in or near where Mr Trevanion's sluice lately stood, which is about 50 foote different from where the antient headweare stood and have permitted the water to overflow Golden Moore … to the great damage of the plaintiff for erecting of which new headweare and for permitting Golden Moore in Cuby to overflow this action is chiefly brought …"[15]

The site of Tregony Mill lies at the end of Mill Lane, which drops steeply down from the village to the "moore", the marshy flood plain of the Fal. Here it is joined by an ancient sunken trackway, "Mucky Lane" Back Lane in 1787 which provided access to the moor from the northern outskirts of the village. A public footpath to the right (north) in a short distance takes one past a spring in a rock-cut basin, to climb up onto the mill platform, or what is left of it, several metres above the flood plain. The only possible remnants of a mill building consist of slaty rubble on the edge of the platform. One might conclude that the mill was a timber building, which would have extended out beyond the platform. There is the semblance of a tail race in the form of a ditch through the marshy ground towards the river. The 1787 map of Tregony depicts the plan of the mill and races, the river then being quite wide here. This may have been caused by the river being "backed up", by a head weir across the channel, raising levels for water to run into a leat on the western side for Nansaker Mill, further down the river. This head weir is depicted on the later Cuby tithe map.

The leat for Tregony Mill, one and a half miles in length, is shown clearly on the 1880 large scale O.S. map. It begins in a waterside meadow about 600 yards upstream from Golden Bridge. Access is via a "permitted path" which can eventually take one to Creed church. The nearby River Fal runs swiftly in a deep narrow channel, its surface two or three metres below the level of the meadow. It can be heard rather than seen: the banks are densely lined with mature trees, particularly alder. We are at the site of Norden's Hayle-Boat-Rock; Melchisedeck Libbye's Holbert, where, according to seventeenth century depositions, there was a rock to which boats could be tied (see Appendix). H. Michell Whitley, at a meeting of the Royal Institution of Cornwall in January 1881, stated that he had examined the rock, not finding any holes for iron rings on it. A recent personal investigation found that at a short distance upstream of Golden Bridge there was the exposed strata of the underlying killas rock in the bed and bank of the river. If there was ever a prominent rock exposed on the riverside it now may be covered by flood deposition of china clay alluviam.

The Tregony Mill leat begins as a deep ditch at the junction of the river and a tiny tributary flowing from the high ground to the east. The tributary has several branches, one of which passes by a farm, named on the modern map as Halbote. The leat leads southwards as a deep ditch within the line of a mature hedge, following the low contour on the eastern edge of the flood plain. It passes under the easterly track leading to Golden Bridge and Mill. Then, still in a hedge-line, the leat runs along the edge of meadowland once known as "Halbote Moor". Further on it is hidden amongst trees, scrub and marshy ground; after nearly a mile along a public footpath through meadow and woodland, Tregony may be seen in the distance. The path has followed the course of the river and now hugs the eastern edge of the meadow to Tregony. Approaching the mill platform, the path is on an apparently natural raised berm or shelf above the marshy meadow. In theory the leat should be on this berm, having to take water to the top of an overshot wheel. But there is no sign of it, not even a depression. Perhaps it has been lost through hill-wash and the movement of cattle. In about 1700 it was stated that the river was the boundary between Cuby and Probus parishes. The entire length of the leat is now marked on modern maps as the boundary, the river's meanderings obviously making it an unreliable permanent border.

6. *Tregony*

The village of Tregony stands overlooking the valley of the River Fal about 6 miles above its confluence with the main deep navigation channel at Tolverne. It sits on top of a steep-sided spur or ridge of rock on the eastern side of the Fal flood plain. The village is separated from the main bulk of the Roseland plateau by a deep ravine-like valley, one of many carved out by rushing waters during the Ice Age. A small tributary now flows down this valley, joining the Fal at the base of the ridge. Therefore the top is defended on three sides by its natural geography, apart from the level approach from the north. This would have made it an obvious choice for a prehistoric settlement, although very few early artefacts, such as from the Bronze or Iron Ages, are known from the area. Being in a sheltered position close to tidal waters, the valley would have been a rich hunting ground for fish and fowl; in summer the water meadows would have provided good grazing, and the fertile Roseland soil was easily cultivated. The Roman-British period is represented by little more than a possible funerary enclosure and a small amount of pottery, recently excavated from a site on the north side of the village. Nothing is known of the native population that must have lived and worked the land here for the following few hundred years.

In the Domesday Survey of 1086 Tregony is listed as being held by Frawin from Count Robert of Mortain. It was only valued at 15 shillings, therefore was of very little worth to him. Only 3 villeins, 6 bordars and 5 slaves lived there, probably in simple cob cottages near the base of the ridge. Livestock consisted of 3 cattle, 40 sheep and 20 goats. There were 12 acres of woodland and 100 acres of pasture. There were 5 ploughlands and 2 plough teams (oxen). The curving boundaries of the medieval strip fields on the west side of the present village are an important visible feature of Tregony's historic past.

The Manor of Tregony is said to have been gained in about 1176 by Henry, son of Joseline de Pomerai of Berry Pomeroy in Devon, through his marriage to an illegitimate daughter of King Henry I and sister of Reginald, Earl of Cornwall. In 1189 the newly crowned King Richard I embarked on a new crusade to the Holy Land. This encouraged his younger brother, John, to think about attempting to seize the crown. He was supported by a number of barons, including Henry de Pomeroy. One of his exploits, in 1194, was to occupy St Michael's Mount, which was then a monastery, on behalf of John. It must have been about this time that, in the true tradition of his Norman forebears, he raised the defensive works of a motte and bailey castle on the southerly brow of the ridge of rock where the hamlet of Tregony stood.

When Richard's crusade failed, other commitments relating to his French possessions, and imprisonment by the Emperor Henry VI kept him away from England for years. He was to die in France in 1199 after bring struck by an arrow during a siege. John naturally succeeded him. Although heavily taxed, England had not suffered during Richard's absence, said to be due to the government administration set up earlier by his father, Henry II. The population was growing; agriculture and trade improved and wealth increased. Charters were granted to enable new borough towns to be established; one of these was Tregony. Under new more stable regimes the castle eventually became redundant, the Pomeroys apparently building a mansion nearby. The castle motte or mound remained as a ruin for several hundred years.

There are no descriptions of the castle surviving from the short time it was in use. One can only guess at its appearance and function by using other examples of the contemporary motte and bailey castle design, of which there are many. The earliest brief description is that by the antiquarian John Norden, who, in about 1600, wrote: "… the ruins thereof yet speak as they lie altogether on top of a mound".

The basic structure seems to have been a small mound of "Christmas pudding" shape. It was constructed by using earth and rock dug from a deep circular defensive ditch around the base. From Norden's description, there had been a stone-built tower constructed on top, probably containing limited living accommodation for the Pomeroy family and a very small garrison. This would only have been in use during times of conflict. There was probably an outer bailey, consisting of a bank and ditch, as a first line of defence. The steep sides of the ridge also provided defence, apart from the northern approach.

Although there were later civil conflicts, the Pomeroys seem to have soon lost interest in their castle. As the structure crumbled away over the years, the site was robbed of stone to build local cottages. In 1699 a lease between landowner Hugh Boscawen and blacksmith Richard Jolilfe (possibly Joliffe) refers to a dwelling house and two ground rooms adjacent to the castle wall. This may refer to an outer bailey wall. The 1787 map of Tregony shows that the mound, situated beside the "Tregony Hill" road, and south of the later almshouses, was completely clear of buildings. There is no indication of the early priory or later mansion that are supposed to have been originally near the castle.[16]

The remnants of the castle were surveyed and sketched in 1862 by Dr C.J. Bennetts and Stephen Roberts of Tregony and a report deposited in the Cornwall Record Office.[17] Some of the text is confusing, understandably considering what the authors were able to see of the ruins. The bounds of a possible bailey were indicated to the north and south of the mound. None of the walls were standing, but a mass of fallen masonry was seen in the north-east part of the rock-cut ditch encircling the mound. That masonry may have been the remnants of a gateway tower. The castle's defensive ditches had long since been filled in with rubbish from the decayed walls. One ditch section was thought to be about 12 feet wide at the top, but the depth apparently not ascertained. The masonry was bonded with lime and sand containing many sea shells. The authors were told that the mound was once up to 40 feet in height. A possible well shaft, full of black earth, was seen in the centre of the top of the mound. When the mound was finally demolished in 1862, for the profit of "certain individuals", the shaft was seen to extend for some distance into the rock below.

Tregony is thought to have received borough status in 1201, granted by the newly-crowned King John. A market area was created on the north side of the castle site, and a wide road, the present Fore Street, extended towards Cuby church (although this church may not have been built until 1267). Burgage plots were laid out on either side of the road consisting of narrower strips on the western side of the road than the east. Dwellings, or shops, faced the road, with working areas, gardens and orchards on the strips at the back. The strips were restricted in their length by the steep slopes of the ridge on which the village stood. The strips are still reflected in the modern property boundaries. The area of the borough was extended northwards towards Cuby church in about 1300. The bridge over the Fal was also first built about this time. Charters were obtained to hold a weekly market and annual fair. The new borough, believed to initially consist of a total of 36 burgesses, was able to send two members to the Parliament of 1295. Later, from 1559, Tregony was represented regularly until the Great Reform Act of 1832. Some well-known local names were represented; such as Henry Pomeroy in 1604, and Hugh Boscawen, the new owner of the manor, in 1679. Tregony became known as a "potwalloper" borough, where voting eligibility depended on the voter being able to boil a pot over his own fireplace. In Tregony's case that could have meant as few as 25 voters. It was also a pocket borough, its eligible (male) householders' votes manipulated by bribe or threat to favour their landlord's candidate for election to Parliament. Corruption peaked in the voting war in 1812, when thousands of pounds changed hands and many tenants faced eviction. After the subsequent enquiry one participant was sent to Newgate Prison. Such boroughs were disenfranchised under the 1832 Act.

Meanwhile a new parish, Tregony St James, had been created out of the southern part of Cuby parish. The early church, dedicated to St James, had been built down on the edge of the flood plain at the foot of the ridge. This proved to be a most unsuitable site. Presumably it was given this ground because space on the narrow ridge above was so limited. Here properties could be leased out, and the Lord of the Manor would reap the profits. As early as 1435 the fabric of the church was in danger, supposedly from flooding and the amount of alluvium washed down the river. It seems to have remained in use until at least 1540 when John Leland visited the area. But only nine years later it had been abandoned and its valuables removed to Cuby church. Thereafter the two parishes were combined.

Practically nothing is known about the early people of Tregony; presumably the greater number were agricultural labourers and their families. They would have lived at little more than subsistence levels, just managing to provide a percentage of their produce to give for church tithes and rent to the Lord of the Manor. An early hint that there were artisans such as cloth makers, or even a higher class of merchant in the town comes from a curious occurrence in 1474. It concerns a John Robert, a Tregony mercer, dealing in high quality textiles, but not necessarily a manufacturer. He had gone to London on business, where he had been persuaded by two gentlemen to give them the sum of £9-2shillings and 6 pence (today's equivalent of about £4,500). This was intended to be a returnable contribution towards a loan being collected for King Edward's expedition to France the following year. Several years later John Robert petitioned the King's Chancellor as the two men had not repaid him on the due date. The result of any subsequent prosecution is not known.[18]

It is not understood why a mercer such as Robert resided in Tregony at that time, apart from the possibility of being a middle man dealing with imports into Penryn or Truro. There are indications that there was some cloth produced locally, but probably only from the tough little "Cornish hair" sheep now believed to be typical of the county at that time. According to a document of 1494 relating to a deed of gift, Sir Richard Pomeroy had two fulling mills in Tregony. He now gifted William Lenne, glover of Tregony, an adjacent parcel of land for the building of a house and fulling mill, with the stream of water flowing through it. It was situated "between a lane coming from Greganwylls on the east and the Sanctuary land of the vicar there on the east".[19] It is unclear if this description refers to the Fal or the stream mentioned below. A "Fulling

A fulling mill in the mid-eighteenth century, by the artist Paul Sandby.

Mill Meadow", situated on the southern edge of the town, is listed on the detailed map of Tregony of 1787 in the Cornwall Record Office. The water to drive such a mill, or mills, would have been taken from the small stream that runs off the Roseland and through the deep picturesque valley on the east side of the town, entering the Fal below the bridge. This is believed by a local resident to have been called "Cary Water". A "Curveigh Water" is given as a boundary to some properties in a terrier of 1680, describing Tregony Church lands.

There are contradictory reports of Tregony's seventeenth century prosperity and population, which in 1660 was said to number 237. A report of 1630 stated that there were 36 alehouses in the town. If true, it seems an extraordinary number, but it would have been a "cottage industry", when small (weak) beer was the staple drink of the common people everywhere. In 1673 the town was noted as "a place much decayed". On the other hand, apart from the general agricultural work, there seems to have been at some stage employment in a successful cloth industry.

Robert Bennett, a Tregony cloth merchant, died in 1607. His will, and the long inventory that went with it, indicates that he could have obtained supplies from abroad.[20] These would have been shipped in through Penryn, already a busy trading town. (The Enys family of Penryn were major importers for much of the century.) Bennett's stock included over 50 types of cloth, lace, canvas and sailcloth. He also became a grocer, dealing in a number of dried fruits, spices, almonds and rice. One imagines that the market for these products was among the most wealthy in the district, including of course his landlord, the Lord of the Manor. Bennett's will doesn't indicate that he actually manufactured cloth in the town. The will of local clothier Francis Betty, who died in 1689, reveals that he also was quite successful; his estate included stocks of serges, yarn and wool. In 1699 the valuers of the estate of Samuel Pentire, valued it at £497; they thought he should be classified as a "gentleman". He had stocks of wool, serges, cloth, fulling tools, oil, iron and coal.[21]

Towards the end of the eighteenth century an attempt was made to improve transport communications in the Roseland district. At that time local dirt roads were only traversed by horses, pack mules, and farm carts. With a growing economy, road improvement was necessary to cater for larger and more frequent horse-drawn vehicles. In 1761 an Act of Parliament was passed to set up the Creed, Tregony and St Just Turnpike Trust. A main turnpike already existed between Lostwithiel and Truro. Improvements were to be made to the road running southwards from a connection with the turnpike road at Hewas Water, to Tregony and Ruan Lanihorne. Similarly, the Trust was also to improve the road from the same turnpike at Denas Water, near Tresillian, to Tregony Bridge and onwards to Trethem Mill, near St Just. The 1787 Tregony map appears to depict a toll gate and possible toll house at the foot of "Tregony Hill", and another gate close by on the eastward approach to the bridge. The roads went through eight parishes and had eight toll gates. Further Acts followed in 1805 and 1827 to "more effectively" improve those roads.

Although Tregony lost its borough status in 1832 its residents continued to refer to it as a town rather than a village. *Pigot's Directory* of 1830 lists a maltster, blacksmith, wheelwright and ironmonger. Its shops on Fore Street and a Saturday market provided goods and services for many townspeople and others visiting from the scattered farmsteads on the Roseland. There were grocers, shoemakers, tailors and drapers. Professional people included a surgeon and schoolmaster. Goods to and from Truro could be carried by William Perryman, whose horse van left his house in Tregony every Wednesday and Saturday. The London Inn, New Inn, Town Arms, and Old King's Arms provided relaxation and sustenance for the working man. All brewed their own beer.

Tregony Clock
Tower, dating
from 1833.

The Tregony
village pump, near
the site of the old
market place.
Looking north
along the wide
Fore Street.

A northern part of Fore Street. The imposing "Old Rectory", was built as a private house in the late eighteenth century. The second building to the right is the ancient King's Arms public house.

During the Victorian Age Tregony's isolated position made it difficult for the population to benefit from the financial advantages brought by the Industrial Revolution. Its young men and women would have had to move away to larger towns or the mining districts. Apart from agriculture, unskilled men might only find work on road maintenance or building projects. One such was the town Clock Tower, dating from 1833. Its construction was funded by a private benefactor. An adjacent small town hall and market house were added by the Borough Corporation, but since removed. It is thought that the original market house stood in the middle of Fore Street. This was possibly near the area known as The Square and in the vicinity of the medieval market place near a theoretical outer bailey of the castle. Another project, towards the end of the century, was the rebuilding of the ancient bridge over the Fal, on a slightly different road alignment. It had proved too narrow to allow the passage of the latest agricultural machinery and road transport.

In 1895 a survey by the Parish Council found that there were 38 unoccupied cottages in the back rows and courts, many of them dilapidated. A leading councillor spoke pessimistically of

The walled causeway to Tregony Bridge.

Tregony Bridge, looking upstream towards the distant wooded Golden Hill. The post on the left is part of the water level recording telemetery system (with a hut on the right off the picture).

Tregony Bridge in the 1920s, the river white with clay waste.

the abject poverty in a rapidly declining village. However, the twentieth century brought an improvement in Tregony's fortunes: *Kelly's Directory* of 1926 lists a similar number of craftsmen and traders as operated here a century before. There were now six shops and a post office, but the emphasis was still agricultural, the community probably comprising many families whose forebears had been there for generations.

The twenty-first century has brought improvements in subjects such as health and education that could not have been imagined by earlier Tregonians. On the debit side, the vibrant village life depicted in Victorian photographs seems to have gone: Fore Street often seems deserted by the populace; with just one remaining pub and one shop and post office, although the road itself is often busy with traffic. The old houses and cottages have been renovated and some small estates built on the northern edge of the village. Most of the occupiers now own their homes, rather than being tied to the Lord of the Manor, as was once the case. The motor car has allowed for an unprecedented country-wide population movement as people in various ways have attempted to improve their lives. Tregony has not escaped the arrival of "incomers", who no doubt appreciate and respect their chosen surroundings, although perhaps not attaining the "sense of identity" of the locals. A number of the village's buildings, some dating from the seventeenth and eighteenth centuries, are now listed as being of architectural and historic value, including the iconic Clock Tower and the alms houses, the latter first built in 1696. Tregonians are fortunate in being able to enjoy the beauty of the Roseland and Fal Valley on their doorstep, and living in a unique historic medieval town, perched on top of its steep-sided ridge, first laid out 800 years ago.

7. Nansaker Mill and Environs

In 1597 the Italian cartographer Giovanni Battista Boazio produced *The True Desscryption of ye Great Baie of Falmouth*, charting in considerable detail the main estuary of Carrick Roads and sub estuaries and the creeks of St Mawes, Penryn and Truro; also the River Fal from its junction with the main river at Tolverne to Tregony. Of course Boazio did not have the advantage of later surveying and cartographic techniques. However, the twists and turns of the Fal are carefully recorded, perhaps over-emphasized, together with the minor creeks such as that at Ruan Lanihorne. Just above, in the vicinity of Lanihorne Wood, is printed "Ruan Lanihorne R or Freshe", which seems to denote that the river is non-tidal. From that point upstream to Tregony Bridge the river meanders through "Moores" and "Moorishe Ground". On the east bank lies "St Margett Chappel" (St Margaret's chapel), depicted as a small building with a twin conical roof. This was part of the now deserted medieval village of Sheepstall, where the house called Porters is shown on modern maps. Opposite, and slightly upstream (actually about 250 metres) on the west side of the flood plain, there is depicted a hip-roofed building with a mill wheel on the side, together with the appellation "Mr. Carmenes Mill". This is Nansaker Mill, or an earlier version of the same. A mill leat is not drawn, but twin tail races are seen rejoining the main river below.

Boazio's chart is incredibly detailed compared, say, to the Greenvile Collins' Falmouth Harbour chart of 1693, which is much more simple in style: beyond Ruan his only feature before Tregony is "Fluce" (sluice), a possible representation of the mill. From the navigational aspect, Collins marks a depth of 3 fathoms, plus anchorage symbols, opposite Mill Creek

THE FAL CHANNEL AND MILL LEATS AT TREGONY CIRCA 1840

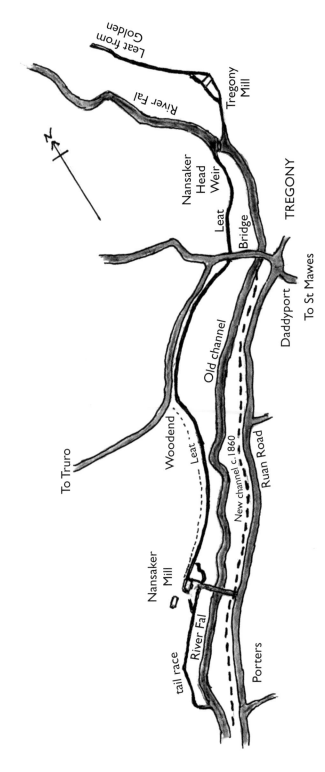

Leat from Golden

River Fal

Tregony Mill

Nansaker Head Weir

N

Leat

Bridge

TREGONY

To St Mawes

Old channel

Daddyport

To Truro

Woodend

Leat

New channel c.1860

Ruan Road

Nansaker Mill

tail race

River Fal

Porters

Sketch map based on the Veryan, Cornelly and Cuby tithe maps, circa 1840.

near the confluence with the main river, and only half a fathom (3 feet) of water above Ardevora, the wide expanse of water approaching Ruan Lanihorne.

Using today's Ordnance Survey measurements, Nansaker Mill was situated half a mile below Tregony Bridge. We do not know when it was first built; it could have been any number of decades previous to 1597. Leland, in about 1540, stated that the tide reached to a quarter of a mile from the bridge. A mill wheel will not turn if its bottom paddles or buckets are immersed in water, such as at Leland's supposed high tide, if the mill existed then, a most inefficient circumstance. In that case Leland must have been wrong: the average tide could not have reached the mill. Boazio seems to previously confirm this by describing the river in the vicinity of Lanihorne Wood as "Freshe".

Nansaker Mill is obviously operating in 1686, being mentioned in Exchequer Depositions in the dispute between the two Trevanion cousins, discussed elsewhere: the supply of water to

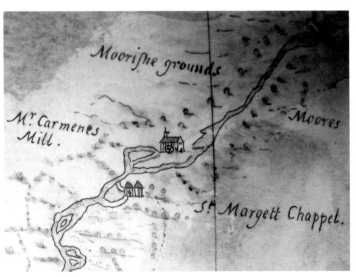

Detail from the Boazio chart of 1597, depicting Nansaker (Mr Carmenes) Mill and St Margaret's Chapel at Sheepstall (Porters).

Nansaker in about 1790, depicting the mill and mill house, leat to the back of the mill, overflow and tail races. Part of the course of the river is seen below. Detail from a map of Woodend Tenement. (Cornwall Record Office G/1884).

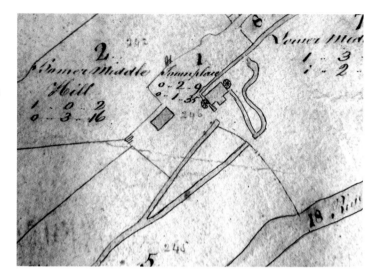

the mill had been interfered with by the attempts of Charles Trevanion of Crego to make the Fal navigable up to and beyond Tregony. Although the mill was on the Trewarthenick estate of Cornelly Parish it was owned at that time by Charles Trevanion of Caerhays estate on the coast to the east. Trewarthenick had been purchased by the Gregor family in 1640.

The Gregor estate archives contain a few copies of leases issued by the Trevanions to Nansaker millers: on 25 December 1771 a lease was drawn up between Ann Trevanion, widow, late of Caerhays and now living in Pembrokeshire, and two millers: Simon Libby of the parish of St Just and Henry Pardew of Ruan Lanihorne. The lease included the mill house, watercourses, headweir, flood gates, and portions of land associated with the leat system. It did not include timber and mineral resources such as tin and copper. The rent, presumably annual, was £140. The children of the millers were also mentioned: Mary Libby, 13, John Libby, 11, Elizabeth Pardew, 10 years of age. The mill had formerly been occupied by Henry Edwards and Robert James.

In 1805 Nansaker Mill, plus various lands on Cornelly parish, was owned by "John Trevanion Parnell Bettesworth Trevanion, esq", presumably living at Caerhays. He now leased the property to William Jenkin Roberts of Ruan Lanihorne. The previous miller had been James Behenna. In 1827 the leasing of the mill, which had been occupied by Roberts, seems to have been handed over by Trevanion to Gordon William Francis Gregor of Trewarthenick.

By 1838 Gregor leased the mill to miller James Fisher, born at Mevagissey in 1806; his wife Elizabeth was born the same year at Veryan. Four of their six children are recorded as born in Cornelly, very likely at the mill house. However, the family left the mill early in 1844; Fisher is recorded in the 1851 census as a miller in Kea parish, therefore probably at Penpol Mill. By 1871 he had moved to two other mills.

The Cornelly tithe apportionment of 1844 lists Nansaker Tenement being now occupied by Charles Paddy. The property included the mill house, yard, garden and a few acres of arable on Middle and Trelask Hill, probably land on the steep hill behind the mill. There were also a few acres of pasture on Lower, Middle, and Higher Moors, being the flood plain meadows towards Tregony Bridge. Also included was "waste by headware", a small piece of ground where the mill leat left the Fal close to Tregony Mill. This was a vital condition of the lease, allowing the miller access to the head weir sluices to adjust the flow of water to the mill.

Charles Paddy was born in St Just (probably in Roseland) in about 1811. His wife, also called Elizabeth, was born in 1816 at Tregony. They probably married and first lived there, for their first child was born in the village in 1836. Paddy must have been an apprentice miller locally; he was miller at Trelucky Mills on the Portholland stream in 1841 before taking over Nansaker in 1844. Three of their six children were to be born at the mill, the last there being Charles, in 1847. Nansaker is absent from the 1851 census return. Paddy had moved by then to Higher Mill, Veryan, and later to Portholland. After 1844 any Nansaker miller would have found it difficult to keep the mill wheel turning. The leat across the flood plain was receiving inundations of china clay waste, particularly during winter river spates. The 1880 O.S. map shows that the leat from the river down as far as the bridge causeway no longer existed, apart from acting as a field drain; the mill could no longer operate. An improving transport system and the availability of flour ground at modern roller mills at Truro and elsewhere meant that small mills such as Nansaker were gradually becoming redundant.

The Gregor Trewarthenick archives contain a detailed map of "Hills alias Nansaker Mills and Woodends Tenement", believed to date to about 1790. It shows the meandering course of the river and straighter mill leat below the bridge causeway. The leat runs close to the western edge of the flood plain, past Woodend to the mill, an estimated distance of about half a mile from where it passes under the causeway. The plan of the mill is drawn with two wheels, at right angles to the leat, on either side of the building. A leat overflow channel and two tail races are also shown.

The Cornelly tithe map shows the full length of the leat, beginning at the head weir on the river close to Tregony Mill. The total distance is only about three quarters of a mile. This leads one to speculate about the gradient of the land surface and leat when the mill was working; there had to be a sufficient "head" of water to turn the wheels. Today the river itself is certainly running at a good rate as it passes downstream through the bridge. The question arises as to the type of wheels used on the mill.

An overshot wheel requires a head of water of at least 15 feet (4.5m) to operate. As the course of the leat was so short at that location it did not give a sufficient fall to operate that type of wheel. An undershot wheel requires little fall, but a good continuous force of water to drive it round. A small leat may not have had the capacity for that, and the position of the wheels is wrong. The third type, the breastshot wheel, may have been used. This requires a minimum head of six to seven feet (2.0m), which must have been achievable here: water is fed from a sluice gate to strike the bucket-type paddles at about wheel axle height. This same system must have been used to drive the mill for several hundred years.

The china clay industry, based around the headwaters of the Fal and St Austell rivers, was to cause serious pollution problems for more than a century. During the extraction and refining processes vast quantities of ground water were used. For every ton of refined clay produced there is estimated to have been between five and nine tons of waste material. Apart from the materials stored in the famous "Cornish Alps", much of it, in suspension, was allowed to drain into the rivers. The amount may be gathered from the annual clay production figures: half a million tons by the year 1900, and rising. Belated legislation to stop the clay effluent polluting the river was introduced in about 1960. The flood plain must have received many layers of that alluvial material when the river broke its banks during winter spates. But generally the white flowing river carried its load of sand, mica and clay to deposit it further down the valley where it settled as it met the tide. The depth of waste in the vicinity of Tregony is not known; the white mole hills that dot the riverside moors between here and Grampound can only indicate that these poor creatures are digging through at least the top foot or so of this sterile material.

Probably from when it was first used, the little riverside road from Tregony to Ruan Lanihorne has been subject to flooding when the sea has backed up the river during exceptionally high spring tides. Under an Act of 1762 the road came under the

care of the Creed and St. Just Turnpike Trust. On 16 February 1854 the turnpike trustees wrote to the proprietors of the clayworks company of St Stephen and St Dennis for reparation because of flooding of the road, allegedly due to the deposition of sand and gravel brought down the river. (At the time the river below Tregony Bridge meandered across the middle of the flood plain down towards Ruan.) Apparently the County Council had agreed to pay towards improvements to the river and Tregony Bridge. Lord Falmouth and owners of the lands above the bridge were to be asked for contributions. Specifications were to be made for a new cutting of the river channel below the bridge. A further letter on 14 April 1855 intimates that costs of £400 were to be obtained from the clay company. Notices would be placed in the *West Briton* and *Royal Cornwall Gazette* asking for tenders for the work. No further information on the proposed scheme has been found, but the major operation was obviously carried out.[22]

The 1843 tithe map shows that the Fal below Tregony Bridge still followed its natural meandering course towards the western side of the flood plain. However, the 1880 Ordnance Survey Map reveals that there had been major earth-moving works undertaken in the intervening years. The ancient meandering channel has disappeared, to be replaced by a new river course closely parallel to the Ruan road, where it has remained to this day. The little "Carey Water" stream which originally flowed into the Fal just below Tregony Bridge, was diverted into a new narrow channel between the road and the new course of the river. It now enters the river at a considerable distance downstream.

The 1880 map also shows that the Nansaker Mill building and the lower part of the leat and mill race were still there to be recorded. The building was not depicted on the 1908 map, but the ditches of the watercourses are still shown. So it seems that there had been no serious inundation of china clay waste to

Opposite page, top: The white flooded valley near Porters in October 1924. A County Council photograph in the Cornwall Record Office, (CC/5/3/12).

Bottom: River meanders below Porters. Sheep graze where tin streaming once took place. Old deposits of clay waste are exposed in the banks.

bury them. The absence of the building at that time means that there may be doubt over Peter Gilson's statement (*The Upper Fal*, 1994) that only the roof still projected above the clay waste deposits. He didn't say if this was from personal observation or hearsay. There is a need for core sampling or a geophysical survey to clear up the matter!

The slope of the steep hill behind Nansaker Mill must have once continued nearly vertically down to the valley floor. However, centuries ago a narrow shelf was cut away near the base, forming a level track from the public road at Woodend to the mill. This provided the route for grain to be carried in and ground cereals out, as well as materials for the working of the mill. It of course provided access for the miller and families living there.

The track also served, at least by the early nineteenth century, as a way for people and animals to cross the valley at that point, over the mill races and a bridge across the river, to join the Tregony to Ruan riverside road. This is clearly seen on the 1813 one inch Ordnance Survey Map and Veryan and Cornelly tithe maps. It has been previously stated, by Henderson and others, in studies of the deserted village of Sheepstall on the east bank, that an ancient road from the east crossed the valley there. The very steep hill on the Cornelly side may have been negotiated via a narrow, probably very wet, combe opposite to Sheepstall. The travellers may have had problems with the incoming tide if, as it was also stated, that in earlier times it ebbed and flowed above that point ! The Nansaker route was a drier alternative.

Nansaker was not the only water-mill to have once operated in that vicinity, albeit not on the main river. M. L. Somerscales, in *"Short Notes"*, *Cornish Archaeology*, Volume 3, 1964, quoting Henderson, gives details of an early corn mill and fulling mill at Sheepstall. The mills were referred to in legal documents regarding a dispute at "Shepestalle juxta Tregoni" in 1291. This is an early date for both types of mill in Cornwall. Water was said to derive from a very small stream which runs into the Fal below Sheepstall. It is not much more than half a mile in length, rising from springs on the hillside behind Sheepstall. It seems too small to have given a regular supply to the mills. Perhaps geological or climatic conditions were more suitable at that period.

Almost opposite, across the valley in Cornelly parish, lies the small ancient farm house and estate of Trelasker. It adjoins the larger estate of Trewarthenick. A Stephen de Trewerthenec is mentioned in fourteenth century documents; in 1341 he gifted tenements in Trewarthenick and Tregony to Roger Collyn,Vicar of St Anthony.[23] In the mid-fifteenth century the estate was owned by John Trenowyth. He was descended from a John de Trenowyth, recorded in the reign of Henry II. The family had close connections with the manor of Ventongollen in the nearby parish of Merther. There is a memorial brass to John Trenowyth, dated 1498, in St Michael Penkevil church.

In 1479 Trenowyth decided to harness the power of a diminutive stream in a steep valley on the boundary of the above estate to operate a fulling mill, just as had been done at Sheepstall many years before. The course of the leat he proposed happened to run over the Trelasker property. Accordingly he wrote to the owners for permission to use that route. He may have approached them with some trepidation, for one was perhaps one of the most famous, even notorious, people in the land. Why he owned this small house in the middle of nowhere is difficult to understand, unless as a bolt-hole during those uncertain times. According to the transcript of a document in the Gregor Trewarthenick archives, in 1479 Trelasker was owned by "Sir Henry Bodrugan, Sir Thomas Vaughan and others". These two named gentlemen were prominent supports of King Edward IV during the Wars of the Roses. Bodrugan is one of the most well-know of the Robber Barons of the time; confusingly, he was also a Trenowyth, having taken the name of his house and estate of Bodrugan, overlooking the spectacular Chapel Point, near Mevagissey.

Vaughan had held high office for many years; in 1478 being elected to Parliament as Knight of the Shire for Cornwall. Although named in the document, it is impossible to know if these important men were actually at Trelasker, attending to such a mundane domestic matter. They were more likely to have been concerned about their options on the future of the Crown. King Edward was to die in 1483; the same year the supporters of his successor, Richard III, captured and murdered Vaughan. Bodrugan had changed his allegiance to Richard, but with the king's death at Bosworth only two years later had to run for his life to exile in Ireland. Both men may have wished that they had spent less time on matters of State, and more time on their estate matters, such as that in 1479:

> "Sir Henry Bodrugan Sir Thos Vaughan and others grant permission to John Trenowyth Esq. Lord of the Manor of Trewarthenick full power to make a ditch or mill leat in their land of Trelasker on the east side of the farm so as to supply his fulling mill of Trewarthyneck. Dated at Trelasker 4 July 19 Ed IV."[24]

8. Ruan Lanihorne and the Fal to Tolverne

Not far from Porters the Ruan road climbs up to a height of 70 metres, allowing grand views across the rich Roseland soils; the river lies below, out of sight in its deep valley. There is no room for a road beside the river on the valley floor: the hills drop too steeply onto the narrow flood plain on both sides, a reminder of the Ice Age torrents that originally cut the channel. Therefore the hill has to be climbed, into and out of Ruan. The Gregor canal scheme previously noted tells us that by the eighteenth century the valley floor had filled up with natural and mining alluvium for some distance towards the reach of normal high tides, allowing some useable pasture to develop upstream of the inter-tidal marsh. The construction of Sett Bridge and its causeway in 1883 inevitably accelerated this. The Fal meanders across this flood plain before rushing through the five rounded arches of the bridge. But it has to give way to the incoming high tide flooding back up through the bridge, for less than half a mile today on an average tide. Downstream, the further 2 miles of water to the confluence with Truro River at Tolverne are designated on the navigation chart as Ruan Creek, although that title is more appropriate for the nearby short branch to Ruan Lanihorne village.

The few houses, public house, and medieval church of Ruan Church town are perched on the side of a steep south-facing slope overlooking the little tidal Ruan River. The manor was held from post-Norman times by the Archedekne family (the spelling of the name varies), who had their isolated mansion where the village now stands. According to the *Calender of Patent Rolls*, on 31 January 1335 Baron John Archedekne, like his father before him a supporter of Edward III, was granted a

Upstream view from Sett Bridge at high tide.

Sett Bridge, built in 1883.

licence to crenellate "his dwelling place". In other words, to either fortify his existing mansion or build a new castle. Later reports that there may have been a round keep on the site may indicate an earlier fortification.

John seems to have spent a great deal on a new stone structure, covering a large area of the slope down to the creek side. Leland was later to say that it originally had seven towers. The reason for the necessity for such a large castle here is unclear. But this was at the beginning of the Hundred Year's War; Edward would be trying to fortify the South Coast against French incursion. However, a garrison at this location would be unlikely to help to defend the Fal estuary ports of Truro and Penryn.

Although remote, the castle could have been victualled by boat from Truro, depending on the tide. Otherwise provisions could have been brought by packhorse over the hill from the Archedekne village of Shepestall where, in 1334, John had been granted a charter for a weekly market and annual fair.[25] A necessary manorial corn mill may have also been operating on the nearby Ruan River by this time.

John Archedekne died in 1378, being succeeded by his son, Warin, who was knighted, presumably for services to the monarch. He died in 1400, leaving three daughters by his wife Elizabeth. The eldest, Alienore, married Sir Walter de Lucy, who inherited the castle. However, owning other estates, he had no interest in the property which, probably with enormous overheads, would prove to be a white elephant. It quickly fell into ruin: over the years it became a quarry and a source of timber; many of the village houses that replaced it were probably built from the materials.

Boazio's chart of 1597 features the two remaining towers, said to be 50 feet in height. They stand together facing the

The church and
castle at Ruan
Lanihorne.
Detail from the
Boazio chart of
1597.

creekside, possibly with an arched entrance between them. The
last tower was said to have been demolished in 1718. The
nearby village church survived all the years of disruption on its
doorstep. Boazio depicts a small steeple on top of the tower.
This may have fallen down in 1658. The little building,
dedicated to Saint Rumon, in spite of a number of alterations
including "Victorianization", stands as a beautiful example of
a medieval village church.

The Rev John Whitaker, Rector of Ruan and noted historian,
writing in 1791, even before the addition of large amounts of
china clay waste, was concerned about the build-up of alluvium
in the creek, polluting the shellfish beds and restricting the
navigation channel. In the mid-eighteenth century the village
and district was supplied with Welsh coal, timber and other
goods, brought by small coasting vessels of up to 100 tons, to a
wharf and coal yard close to the village. However, by the time
of his writing, Whitaker says that within living memory the coal
vessels had to lay aground off Kiln Point, Lamorran, to unload
their cargoes. More recently these vessels had been replaced by
smaller single-master sloops, probably flat-bottomed Fal barges.

Ruan Lanihorne church.

The adventurous barge crews managed to struggle up to Ruan Quay over the next century, through waters coloured a milky white by the china clay waste. A quay had been built further down the creek from the village, providing a landing for small vessels. Peter Gilson, in *The Upper Fal*, stated that cargoes were carried up to Ruan into the 1930s. His book carries a photograph of barge *Eclipse* laying on the mud there. About the same time William Blamey operated a twice weekly ferry service to Truro and other places on the Fal estuary. He first used a steam boat and later a motor launch, using dinghies as boarding tenders where necessary.

The nineteenth-century trade directories give almost a sense of feudalism in their descriptions of the parish: tenants had to pay their rents to landowners such as the Bishop of Exeter (anciently owner of Penryn), mining baron Sir William Lemon, and Lord of the Manor Francis Gregor of Trewarthenick. The parish had a population of about 400, spread among the

Fal barge *Eclipse* on the mud in Ruan Creek, looking towards Lamorran, probably in the 1930s. (Royal Cornwall Polytechnic Society.)

isolated farms and village, known as Churchtown. Here services were supplied by one shopkeeper, a general merchant, butcher, shoemaker and blacksmith. Other supplies had to be sought at Ruan High Lanes, a mile and a half walk away up a steep hill. Towards the end of the century there were enough children in the parish to require a small school for boys and girls. It was situated at the eastern end of the village, close to the smithy and water-mill.

Being so isolated, the parish would have needed its own mill, probably established at an early date, to produce flour and perhaps animal feed milled from locally-grown rye, barley or wheat. The mill was sited at the confluence of the little Ruan River and normal high tide in Ruan Creek. It had an overshot wheel; its leat ran parallel to the little river, down a narrow valley to a mill pond. From there, water was taken via a sluice and launder to the top of the wheel.

The earliest known legal document relating to Ruan Mill is dated 20 May 1649. It relates to a bargain and sale of the mill within other local property, from Robert Wollop, of Farley Wallop, Hampshire, to Truro merchant Thomas Kendall. The property included half of the manors of Ruan Lanihorne and Lanihorne Mill, Lanihorne Wood, plus Melinsey Higher and Lower Mill, Veryan.[26] By 1774 Sir John Molesworth had become the owner; on the 14 December he sold the lease to Nicholas Blamey, gent, of Lanihorne, possibly living at Gonitor, a property in the northern part of the village.[27] On 1 February 1799 Daniel Blamey of Gonitor sold to Francis Glanville and Francis Gregor: the sale included part of the demesnes, the mill, and other property in the village, including half of the castle,possibly for the disposal of the stonework.[28] An 1825 valuation of Ruan Lanihorne named the occupier of the mill and mill house as Edward Pierce.

High tide near the coal wharf in Ruan Creek in the early twentieth century. The man is sculling a typical small working boat. (Royal Institution of Cornwall.)

According to the available trade directories, in 1856 and 1862 the miller was David Pearce. But by 1878 he had probably died, for the mill was being run by his wife Thomasine. She was there for at least ten years, running a shop at the same time, By 1910 James Coad had taken over, but by 1923 he in turn must have died; the succeeding miller was also his wife, Elizabeth. Between 1930 and the beginning of the Second World War John Bassett Coad, possibly a son, had replaced her. No later records have been found. However, the mill at Ruan Lanihorne had outlived many other similar mills.

At Sett Bridge, around high water, the view southwards towards Tolverne is of a vast inland lagoon. It is flanked on either side by the tree-clad slopes of Lamorran and Trelonk, the latter noted for the chimney of the defunct brickworks and the entrance to Tuckingmill Creek. In the distance the view is blocked by the high bulk of Ardevora Veor, a prominence that sqeezes the outgoing river into a narrow winding channel. Once through, it is released into a long exquisitely tranquil lake, fringed to high tide level by ancient tangled oak woodland, all the winding way to Tolverne. Before these lower tidal reaches were affected by clay pollution, generations of local folk trapped migratory fish and raked their managed beds for cockles, mussels and oysters. These were sold commercially or perhaps supplemented their familys' sometimes meagre diet.

The quay below Ruan. The view across the salt marsh towards Ardevora nearing high tide.

Swans graze on eel grass at Trelonk. The chimney marks the site of old brickworks that utilized china clay waste.

Sandbars at Lamorran; the tide is on the ebb.

But back at Sett Bridge, as the tide ebbs the mud flats of the saltmarsh begin to appear. They consist of a combination of natural alluvium augmented by tin streaming and mining waste, finally topped by china clay waste deposits. All were brought down the river over many centuries, to settle in the calm brackish inter-tidal waters of the creek. The mud flats are covered by a rich variety of grasses and rushes, with invading reed beds and willow and alder scrub on the fringes. The whole area has become a rare and wonderful natural habitat of scientific importance.

At low tide the River Fal has an entirely different appearance: from Sett Bridge to Tolverne it is no more than a small stream wending its way haphazardly through mud banks, sand and shingle bars. No general study of the depth of the alluvium has been made. The late Bob Acton, in *Around the Fal* (1994) was told that, at an unknown date, miners attempting to stream for tin close to Lamorran found china clay waste to a depth of 49 feet (15m). This is unlikely, as the clay would have had to be deposited well below low tide levels. Very expensive dredging techniques would be needed to work at that depth.

The rocky foreshore near Mill Creek at low tide.

Left: Autumn oakwoods and low tide sandbars near the confluence with the main river.

Overleaf: The Greenvile Collins chart of 1693, depicting the Fal Estuary (northern section)., The Truro and Tresillian Rivers are to the upper left and the Fal to Tregony to the right.

Let us hope that any future enterprise of a similar nature will be adjudged to be economically and environmentally unsound. These idyllic reaches, now much recovered from past pollution, should be left to the wading birds, herons and kingfishers, and the trout and migrating salmon that are gradually returning to these waters, and, of course, otters. When the tide allows, adventurous boaters may explore these tranquil reaches of the River Fal for centuries to come.

Tolverne; the narrow entrance to the tidal Fal is in the middle distance.

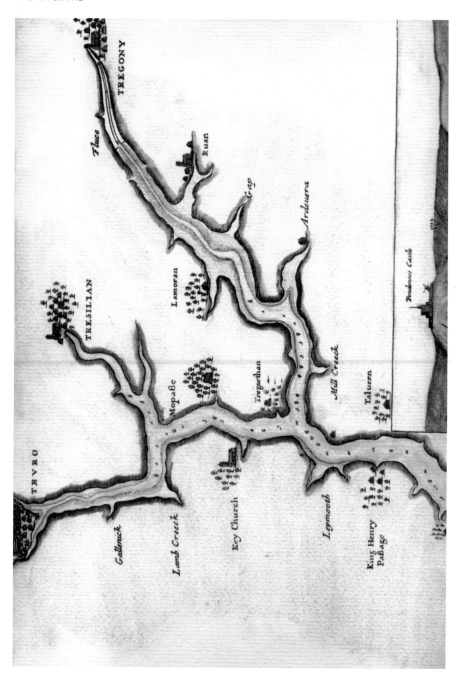

Appendix

The Fabled Port of Tregony

The antiquarian John Leland is believed to be the first "foreigner" to personally visit and describe in considerable detail the County of Cornwall. He travelled around the region in 1542 as part of his topographical study of England and Wales, making copious notes as he went. These were not properly compiled, edited and published until the eighteenth century, forming part of what is known as Leland's *Itinerary*. His description of the environs of the Fal are particularly comprehensive, detailing everything from shipping, the tin coinage at Truro, the market at Penryn, and seals that, as today, occasionally haul out to bask on Black Rock in Falmouth Harbour. The various creeks are described: with respect to the upper reaches of the Fal, he takes us to Ruan Lanihorne and its ruined castle, passing Ardevora and Lamorran, thence:

> "The maine stream goith up 2 miles above Moran Creke, ebbing and flowing, and a quarter of a mile above is the market Toune of Tregony, where is a bridge of stone *aliquot arcuum* (of several arches) apon Fala Ryver. Here is an old Castel and a paroch chyrch of S. James standing yn a more by the Castel..."

All of Leland's distances obviously must be approximations. The Ordnance Survey distance, following the course of the river, from Lamorran Creek to a quarter of a mile from Tregony Bridge, is about 3 miles. Nevertheless, if we accept his findings, at that time the tide, presumably at springs, came up the river to within a quarter of a mile from the bridge. The position of Nansaker Mill, in relation to this was discussed in Chapter Seven. The length of the Fal, from its junction with the main navigable channel at Tolverne, to Tregony, allowing for the tortuous winding of its course, is about 6 miles.

Another to write about the county during the sixteenth century was Richard Carew of Anthony, the family estate on the western bank of the Tamar. He was educated at Oxford, and later in London became a member of the Middle Temple and the newly formed Society of Antiquaries. But his home was in Cornwall, his family having close ties with many of the Cornish gentry. In his *Survey of Cornwall*, published in 1602, he was able to write with great authority on all aspects of Cornish life. In his brief coverage of places around the Fal estuary he seems unaware of Tregony's, later supposed, past as a port, noting it as "... the market and incorporate town of Tregony, not specially memorable (in my knowledge) for any extraordinary worth or accident".

Leland's *Itinerary* was generations away from being published when, about fifty years after his visit, another explorer arrived to describe and map the county, perhaps not with the same attention to detail as Leland. This was the antiquarian and cartographer John Norden, who towards the end of the sixteenth century surveyed much of England for his *Speculi Britanniae*. His notes were completed by 1605 but not edited and printed by William Pearson until 1728. In this original first edition the description of Cornwall was laid out by Hundred, places and curiosities in each Hundred put in alphabetical order.

Of towns around the Fal, Truro was described in glowing terms, being a "pretty compacted town, resident to wealthy merchants, most commendable for its neatness of buildings". Tregony, or Tregny, was "a market town and incorporation ... A very poor town graced sometime with Pomeroy Castle, the ruins thereof yet speak as they lie altogether on top of a mount." (The only description of buildings on the motte.) Grampound's residents are described as few and poor. There are no other references to the upper Fal apart from, curiously, under Probus:

"A Parish: here unto this place hath a braunche of Foye
(meaning Fal) haven come with boates; and below
Probus churche is a rock, called Hayle-boate rocke,
wherein to this day are many great iron rynges
whereunto Boates have bene tyed: Now noe show of a
haven, but a little brooke runneth in the valley..."

The Fowey River is miles away, and Halbote, the name of a
farm, corrupted at that early date into "Hayle-boat", lies close
to the River Fal below Grampound and nearly 2 miles from
Probus church. Norden's apt description of the "little brooke"
implies that he actually reached that isolated spot, where he
seems suitably puzzled over the very dubious information
previously given to him by the locals regarding an earlier haven
or harbour.

A century after Norden's perambulations, Halbote, then spelt
Holbert, is featured in the often quoted statement by the eighty
year-old Melchizedeck Libbye. His was one of a number of
depositions made to the Attorney General in 1686 concerning
a dispute between two Trevanion cousins, both called Charles,
one residing at Cregoe, just to the south of Tregony, the other
at the Caerhays estate to the southeast.

After obtaining an Act of Parliament, for some years the Cregoe
Trevanion had been vainly attempting to make the little River
Fal navigable for boats above and below Tregony Bridge, apparently as far as Crowhill in St Stephen parish, by trying to build
earth dams, locks and sluices. Several English canals, such as the
lateral sea canal to Exeter, completed a century earlier, were to
provide a good return to investors. Trevanion may have been of
a mind to create a miniature Cornish version, not worrying
unduly about initial surveying. Crowhill is only 4 miles above
Tregony, but an insurmountable 30 metres above sea level. The
river flow could vary from a winter spate to barely enough to
drive a mill wheel. The whole project was never likely to succeed.

As the work proceeded at Tregony the Caerhays Trevanion brought a legal case against his cousin, alleging that the altering of the river course interfered with the supply of water to his Nansaker corn mill in Cornelly parish. This stood on the west side of the Fal flood plain about half a mile (770m) below Tregony Bridge. Water to drive the wheels was taken from the Fal into a leat via a head weir situated about 300 metres above the bridge. The leat ran across the west side of the flood plain down to the mill; a culvert taking it under the bridge causeway.

The aforementioned Libbye, a witness for the defendant, stated that at his first remembrance salt water flowed upstream to within a quarter of a mile of the bridge. But his father and others had told him that they had known the sea water flowing a mile and quarter *above* the bridge to Holbert, where there was a rock with several iron rings where people tied their boats.

Libbye's description of the rock with iron rings at Halbote is uncannily similar to Norden's. But the latter's work was not to be published until 1728, therefore Libbye could not have seen it. It could have been one of those "old wives tales" that might persist for generations in such a rural setting. The "little brooke" can scarcely support a canoe at low water times. (Although in 1958 a Mr Newman and companions in an outboard engine-powered dinghy managed to fight their way up from Tregony, against the current and over rocks, to reach Grampound.) Other witnesses, for and against the canal scheme, gave depositions, sometimes quoting what their grandfather, or an old man had told them. This included that the sea once went to Grampound, a man once rode on horseback under Tregony Bridge, and that people once went to St James' church by boat when the river flooded. (The church, situated on the low meadow above the bridge, was abandoned in about 1550.)

So, with regard to the modern belief that the sea once lapped the quays of the port of Tregony at some unspecified time in the past, we have to start with those early statements. In the mid-sixteenth century Leland witnessed or was told that the tide only came up to within a quarter of a mile of Tregony. Norden was given the impression that boats once went up to "Hayle Boat Rock". A century later witness Libbye repeats the "Holbert" mooring ring story gathered from his father and others. Daniel Defoe came to Cornwall in the 1720s on his *Tour Through Great Britain*. He found that Truro was a good port for small ships, but could only say that Tregony was a town of very little trade. "Its chief thing is that it sends members to Parliament ... It has a claim to antiquity, and is an appendix to the Duchy of Cornwall ..."

On 10 June 1883 the subject was discussed at a meeting of the Royal Institution of Cornwall by the Secretary, H. Michell Whitley. He said that " it is traditionally stated" that the tide once flowed to Hayle Boat Rock. He then quoted antiquarian William Hals, since described by a modern well-known researcher as "a rather fanciful historian" – "That the sea once flowed above Tregony Bridge is plain *as tradition* and the sea-sand and shells found there inform us." After discussing early charts, Michell Whitley gave the existing heights of the river above high water mark: 17 feet at Tregony Bridge; 35 feet at Hayle Boat Rock; 60 feet at Grampound; 96 feet at Trenowth Mill. After his own examination of the aforesaid rock he failed to discover any holes for rings. Reporting on tin streaming excavations down to bed-rock in the vicinity, he concluded that 22 feet of solid rock would have to be removed before the tide could flow to Hayle Boat Rock. (And, Michell Whitley's measurements seeming to be correct, at 17 feet [5.20m] above sea level at Tregony Bridge, the tide could not have reached anywhere near there either.) Recent searching by this writer found no prominent rock. However, a short distance north of Golden Bridge it was observed that a few layers of the under-lying rock stratum were exposed at a low level in the river bank.

Several major works on the history of Cornwall were published during the first half of the nineteenth century. They include C. S. Gilbert's *The Historical Survey of the County of Cornwall*, published in 1817; Fortescue Hitchens' *History of Cornwall*, published in 1824; and Davies Gilbert's *Parochial History of Cornwall* of 1838. They were the result of considerable academic and topographical research, although the authors or editors, particularly in *History of Cornwall*, often used material collected by earlier antiquaries. These include William Hals (1655-1737), Thomas Tonkin (1678-1742), and the Rev. John Whitaker (1735-1808). These were ground-breakers in historical studies, but sometimes, perhaps with little source material to go on, some tended to expound their own theories, not letting the facts, as we might know them today, get in the way of a good story.

So, with regard to Tregony: in 1817 we see Gilbert stating that Whitaker, who towards the end of his life was rector of Ruan Lanihorne church, considered that Tregony was once the principal seaport belonging to the south coast of Cornwall. Gilbert does say that there, in about 1750, the woollen industry and sale of yarn was carried on with great spirit; five tucking mills worked at the bottom of the town. But at present, he says, it is destitute of trade, wealth and common activity.

Fortescue Hitchens of St Ives was known in Cornwall more as a poet tnan a historian. By 1814 he had collected a quantity of historical information, mainly gleaned from previously published works, in order to produce a new *History of Cornwall*. He approached Samuel Drew, who agreed to edit the book. Unfortunately, Hitchens died that same year. Nevertheless Drew continued with the publication, collecting further material, retaining Hitchen's name as author. Apart from marked quotations the whole of the final text was said to be "in Mr Drew's language". Drew admitted that some of the information might be erroneous, and made the very dubious statement that "As every man is a historian in his own parish, town or village, the peasant is frequently much better acquainted with the facts which exist in his own neighbourhood than the man who has prosecuted his enquiries with diligence ..." The complete work was finally published in 1824. Mr Drew sustaining a heavy financial loss.

The general gist of the entertaining text may be gathered from Drew's, or another's, description of Tregony, as he wanders into the realms of Greek mythology and Ptolemy's *Geography*:

The Fal – "lies like a vast Briareus (octopus-like creature), stretching forth its gigantic carcass on every side, and throwing out its hundred arms into the land around it. Tregony on the main arm, even the dominating river, was denominated Cenia itself, while the harbour was called the mouth of the Cenia, and the southern road of the Romans in Cornwall terminated at this Cenia ... Tregony was thus a town, at a time when Falmouth, when Penryn, when even Truro itself, was not yet in contemplation."

Cenio has been thought by some to be the ancient British name for the Fal. It appears in Ptolemy's *Geography,* the atlas produced by him in the second century AD. He compiled material gathered from across much of the known world, using previous histories and reports from contempory Roman officials, traders and the military. He produced maps, using a latitude and longitude positioning system. The map of Britain depicted on the Atlas is crude, but can be identified as such. The position of the named river Cenio on the south-west peninsula, is roughly where the Fal is situated. The only place name on the map near the Cenio is Voliba. There has been much speculation about the site of this supposed British town, especially with regard to the tin trade.

The writer of *History of Cornwall* may have thought to elaborate on the gist of Ptolemy's *Geography* to declare that

Tregony originated as a Roman town. Few artefacts of the Romano-British period had been found here until recently. In 2006 professional archaeological excavations at a housing development on the northern outskirts of the village revealed part of a rectangular feature dating to the second century AD. The report suggested that it may have been a cemetery enclosure. The few pottery finds included a handled jug and a large Roman-style cooking pot. Both vessels were made of local clay. Three Roman coins have been found in the surrounding area. Further away, two rectangular sites, possibly Roman, have been seen from the air as cropmarks. This is not enough evidence to prove that Tregony was a Roman town.

Inhabitants of the area may have been in contact with Roman or Continental traders arriving by ship into the Fal estuary. The presence of Roman coin hoards close to the river at Malpas and Restronguet Creek may be evidence of this. The "Malpas Hoard" was found in the eighteenth century on the St Michael Penkevil side of the river. It consisted of up to 5,000 third century Roman copper coins. They were probably temporarily left by merchants who had arrived by ship to trade with the locals, their plans obviously going disastrously wrong. Another place where there was the possibility of trade was just across the valley towards the modern Probus. Here there was the defended enclosure of Carvossa. A Roman presence seems to have been there between the years 60 to 130 AD. Apart from local pottery, excavation has produced fine samian tableware, mortaria and amphora. There have been suggestions that Carvossa was Ptolemy's Voliba. However, the site is too small to have been a notable British town. Alternatives might be the great enclosure of Gear, on the Helford River, or even the equally large univallate enclosure of Golden on the upper Fal, the latter so far unexcavated.

The Roman presence in the South West remained very small compared to the rest of the country. The Roman-style "villa" at

Magor Farm, Illogan, found in 1931, is now thought to be a "celtic" copy of a Roman rectangular house. A similar site to Carvossa is at Nanstallon, near Bodmin. This is a small but typically laid out fort only in use in the early years following the Roman invasion of Britain. It was probably abandoned when it was found that the local Dumnonii tribes accepted Roman rule. Another small fort is close to Restormel Castle, on a promontory overlooking the Fowey River, with "finds" similar to those at Carvossa. A larger fort, just within Cornwall's border, dating from the first century, is at Calstock, overlooking the Tamar. Apart from a possible base for the Roman navy, this could have been an administration centre for any Roman military presence needed in the South West, just in case the Dumnonii decided to object to paying any imposed taxes.

Referring back to *History of Cornwall*: the writer, probably using Whitaker's notes, mentions the Hayle Boat Rock story and states "This evidence seems decisive, to prove that the sea originally visited the foot of Tregony town." He gives the useful information that in about 1800 the tide, presumably the average high, reached to about a mile and a half below the town. If correct, that is about two thirds of a mile higher than it does today. The text continues the Roman theme, maintaining that they built one of their "castles" at Tregony, supposing that the "Green Hill", the site of Lord Pomeroy's medieval castle, was a Roman fort. A Roman town is imagined, stretching along the banks of the Fal, and a quay forming an embankment to the river. There is the gradual development of the later town on its promontory and the demise of maritime Tregony due to tin streaming silting: – "(it) ceased to be a seaport town any longer ... its quay was deserted as useless. Its street, its warehouses, and its church, were left to crumble into ruins. The extended suburbs of the town all sunk away. The town shrunk up its hill again ..." All completely fanciful.

Davies Gilbert's *Parochial History of Cornwall* of 1838 was mainly compiled from the earlier researches of Hals, Tonkin and Whitaker. The text includes material on Tregony already used in earlier books, such as the Trevanion dispute, namely the attempts to make the Fal navigable above Tregony, adding: "the place of its old flux and reflux, yet by reason of the great and rapid confluence and washes of the Val river, in the winter season, after the foundation of the walls of those sluices, being made upon mud and osier ground, where the sea was driven back aforesaid, were undermined, fell down, and were completely driven away." The book's compiler later added: "Mr Whitaker has collected everything that can be known *or conjectured* respecting the ancient state, not of Tregony, but of a town or city supposed of great commercial and ecclesiastical importance, which must have stood nearly on the same spot."

One of the most respected Cornish historians in the early part of the twentieth century was Charles Henderson. Yet even he, on occasion, would use previously published material without questioning its veracity. Among his notes, later published as *The Ecclesiastical History of the Western Hundreds*, he gave some interesting details of Tregony's St James church and its vicinity, following it with the Trevanion dispute, Mr Libbye and so forth. He states that it is probable that the tide flowed considerably above it and indeed a tradition existed in the seventeenth century that the churchgoers at one time approached it by boat. (If indeed the tide went beyond the church, situated on the flood plain, one can envisage an ark-like structure that fell and rose as the tide ebbed and flowed.)

Henderson refers to the place name Daddyport, situated on the south side of Tregony, as possible proof that Tregony was a port. He links it with a Daddyport on the Torridge in Devon, where the tide, he says, once flowed, making the case that the same applied to Tregony. Daddyport at Tregony consists of several properties south of the junction with the Ruan Lanihorne and St Mawes roads, over the parish border, which is a stream, and in Veryan parish. It lies about 100 metres from the Fal river bank below the bridge. Franklin Grigg, in his local history book *Tregony Happenings* (2004) wrote that people at the lower end of the town once used a well at Daddyport. An original indenture of 1668 mentioning the place is held at the Cornwall Record Office. It concerns the leasing of properties in St. Mawes and Tregony, where, at the latter, there were five houses in " Daddyport, alias Daddiparte", in Veryan parish.

The Henderson essay entitled *A note on the origin of Cornish Towns* was published in 1935, two years after his untimely death. Within it he stated that Tregony was very ancient and has been claimed as a Roman station:

"Everyone knows that Tregony was once a seaport, although it is now high and dry." – and – "The Great Bridge" of Tregony is mentioned in the deed of 1387. Just below the bridge was a quay, and here ships of considerable burthen could discharge their cargo. The river, however, was silting up owing to the sand and gravel washed down from the moors. By 1600 Tregony had turned its back on maritime affairs. Even the attempt of one Elias Heard to bring a lighter of 12 tons burthen to the grass-grown quay in 1684 was unsuccessful. We are told that the boat in question was laden with 'divers wares – to wit, wines, hops, dry fish, one chest of glasses, 2 grosse of bottles, and other commodityes.' Although urged by horses and ropes, it got no higher than Whidley Moor, half a mile short of the bridge ..."

Unfortunately Henderson does not give the source of the above quote. The date, 1684, coincides with the time Charles Trevanion was attempting to make the Fal navigable. The point the boat reached is not as far as Leland's earlier estimate of the tide reaching a quarter of a mile from the bridge, but more likely to have been the true distance.

The "lighter" was probably a Fal "inside" barge, these were small, flat-bottomed, single-masted vessels unique to the Fal, and were used on the estuary and creeks up until the early twentieth century. Cargoes could include agricultural products, stone, timber, coal, market and household goods; sometimes imports from quays at Falmouth or Penryn, or ships anchored in the estuary. With the help of the tide, the bargemen were used to sailing, punting, rowing or bow-hauling their craft up the creeks to isolated communities. In 1626 there was a government survey of maritime resources, ships and men, in the South West. The bargemen of the Fal were a unique class: 47 were listed; 27 at Feock parish, 15 at Mylor, 3 at Kenwyn, and one each at Kea and St Michael Penkevil.

Frank Halliday's *History of Cornwall* was first published in 1959. The text takes us chronologically from the Ice Age to the twentieth century. With regard to Tregony, he relies on, and indeed embellishes, previous "port" assertions: "In the early middle ages a busy little port at the end of the street, but the gradual silting up of the river ruined its seaborne traffic ..." For the first time we have a supposed approximate date, the early Middle Ages, for the existence of the port of Tregony. Unfortunately no reference is given for the source of his information.

In 1994 the late Peter Gilson, for many years a stalwart of the Royal Cornwall Polytechnic Society, wrote in his book *The Upper Fal*, possibly after referring to Halliday, that "Tregony was an important port in the Middles Ages", and briefly paraphrases some of the earlier writers regarding its demise. He does offer some current information on the site of Nansaker Mill: stating that the roof of the building barely projects above the valley floor, being indicative of the great depth of deposited china clay waste alluvium. He doesn't say if this was from personal observation or hearsay. Recent investigations by the author have found little trace of the mill.

In 1996 a *Church Trails Pack*, a tourist guide, was issued by the North Cornwall Heritage Coast and Countryside Service. In the St Cuby (Tregony) church section the author writes "Tregony was a large port on the River Fal in the Middle Ages until the river silted up and most of its water was diverted for washing tin ... in those days the tide flowed considerably above Tregony Bridge ..." An interesting variation on the general interpretation of events.

In 1997 there appeared *The Fal Estuary Historic Audit*, a comprehensive guide to archaeological and historical sites around the Fal, compiled by the Cornwall Archaeological Unit and published by Cornwall County Council. Describing Tregony, the text of the Survey relies on material taken from Victorian sources previously mentioned here, with little regard to their validity. Unfortunately in the future the *Survey's* Tregony "history" may come to be regarded as gospel by historians and the general public alike, not least by the good people of Tregony. To quote from the *Survey*: "The Fal may have been navigable to Golden Mill;" "the medieval port of Tregony;" "The building of Tregony Bridge in 1300 made it impossible for ships to sail above this point;" "A centre of maritime trade;" with – "numerous ale houses needed to keep visiting sailors happy", etc.

The Internet now provides the opportunity to broadcast far and wide similar accounts in guides on Tregony and the River Fal. John Leland, John Norden and Richard Carew, who in the seventeenth century gave those first descriptions of Tregony, would be most surprised to know what credence, and elaboration, has since been put on the dubious statement by Melchizedeck Libbye in 1686.

At the present time it is generally accepted by most that Tregony lost its port because it silted up at some unspecified time, perhaps in the medieval period. To investigate whether or not ships could once physically reach Tregony, Ordnance Survey maps, contemporary sea level marks and local tidal heights must be considered. There would always have been some natural deposition of alluvium on the flood plain at flood times; further deposition of waste from early tin streaming would not have been excessive compared to that caused by later deep mining and china clay working. As with all rivers, the floor of the valley naturally slopes downwards from source to sea. The angle of the slope varies depending on the underlying geology.

In modern times land heights have been marked at relevant datum points on the larger scale Ordnance Survey maps. On the upper Fal, the first reference point to be considered is the little quay below Ruan Lanihorne, here marked at 3 metres above mean sea level (average half tide). The tidal range in the Fal estuary is approximately 5 metres at high water spring tides. Moving upstream, the next datum height is 4 metres on the valley bottom a mile above Sett Bridge. The 5 metre contour line crosses the valley at Lanihorne Wood. The datum height at Trelasker is 6 metres, and on the flood plain below the Tregony Bridge causeway 9 metres. Above the bridge it is 10 metres, and at Golden bridge 14 metres. The present bed of the fast-flowing river immediately below Tregony Bridge has been measured at between two and three metres below the 9 metre point on the adjacent flood plain. Therefore this is at least 3 metres above the approximate high tide level at Ruan Lanihorne quay, where spring tides occasionally overtop the quay and flood the road.

Exceptional tidal surges have been known to flood further up the valley as far as Porters, flooding the Tregony to Ruan road. One such occasion, in February 2014, was caused by a deep depression with strong easterly winds coinciding with spring tides. Environment Agency readings recorded at the tidal gauge at Newham, Truro, were then up to 1 metre above normal spring high tide levels. That tide, backing up the river channel to flood the road at Porters was a long way from reaching Tregony Bridge and its supposed quays.

It has been suggested that sea levels could have been higher in the medieval period, allowing ships to reach Tregony. Modern studies refute this. At the end of the last Ice Age levels rose rapidly from about 120 metres below present. The rate of rise slowed through the Bronze and Iron Ages, reaching present levels in the Romano-British period. Thereafter they remained relatively stable until the discernable rise in the late twentieth century. There has been no significant change in land movement in the West Country. Higher sea levels would have made medieval fishing villages such as Looe and Polperro uninhabitable.

Truro and Penryn were the main settlements in the Fal estuary in the medieval period, both being on tidal creeks with access for shipping at high tides. Truro is said to have received a charter in about 1166 and another, along with Penryn, in the mid-thirteenth century. The great collegiate church of Glasney was established at Penryn by Walter Bronescombe, Bishop of Exeter, in about 1264, Caen stone for its construction being imported from France. The town developed as a local centre of trade, receiving such imports as salt from Brittany and wine from Gascony.

Truro, at the head of the estuary, developed rapidly: as Cornish tin production increased from the 1330s it was given status as a coinage town, where locally produced tin was assayed. Quays were built and a Customs service introduced. Initially the main exports were tin and hides, possibly going coastwise to London rather than abroad. It was the beginning of the Hundred Years War with France; ships on either side could be subject to attack by enemy privateers. Fowey, the premier port on the south Cornish coast, is said to have been sacked and burnt by the French in 1378. In their turn, Fowey mariners not only attacked foreign ships but also those of the English Cinque Ports.

Falmouth, long before it received a charter in the seventeenth century, was a small hamlet called Smithick in the lee of Pendennis headland. It could offer a haven for ships coming into the estuary due to stress of weather. But even here they could be attacked and plundered by the locals, especially if their cargo was wine.

By the mid-fifteenth century the Falmouth estuary ports were becoming a little more "legitimate"; pilgrim ships could sail from Falmouth to Spain in relative safety; Truro, Penryn and Falmouth each supplied two ships for the King's service. But also, notorious pirates, based in Fowey, could visit Falmouth with little fear of arrest. Their ships were balingers, quite small, from 25 to 60 tons, with one or two masts setting square-rigged sails. They were commonly used around the Channel ports, as were cogs, larger flat-bottomed, high-sided merchant vessels, generally carrying one large square sail.

A medieval merchant ship depicted on the town seal of Kiel, Germany, dated to 1365. It has the basic attributes of a cog: deep hull, stern rudder and single square-rigged sail.

These were the circumstances at the time when the port of Tregony is supposed to have flourished. After a long voyage the master of such a vessel might baulk at the prospect of feeling his way up towards Ruan Lanihorne, or beyond, if there was little financial reason to do so. The sail could not be used because the winds there are blanketed or made fickle by the high tree-clad hills on every side. It would have been necessary for the ship to be piloted and towed or punted up with the tide through the shoals of the narrowing winding passage, which would incur time and labour costs. Transhipping cargo into barges might take it up to the limits of the tide half a mile or so below Tregony Bridge.

But what were the profitable cargoes to be taken in and out of Tregony? In 1337 Edward III's eldest son was created Duke of Cornwall, being endowed with all profits of what became known

The Bremen Cog: a sailing reproduction of a fourtenth-century wreck raised from the River Weser, Germany, in 1962. Dimensions approximately 23 metres long by 8 metres beam. The type of vessel that may have once sailed into Falmouth's Carrick Roads. (Photo Barry Wilson.)

as the Duchy Lands. The document *The Caption of Seisin* was the result of a survey of the profits of those lands, including Customs due and the like from Cornish ports. On the Fal estuary, Truro and Penryn were omitted from the list because the Bishop of Exeter, founder of Glasney College, "... had ursurped to himself the pleas, perquisites and customs of the Port of Falemouth". Under the Honour of Launceston there was coverage of properties held at nearby Grampound, but Tregony was only listed by the fact that "Henry de la Pomeroy holds of the Lord Duke 12 fees there ..." and "There is one weak water mill which used to render yearly 30 shillings."

Perhaps there are glimpses of hope for the advocates of a medieval port of Tregony, although the reasons stated above seem against it. The only references known so far for its possible existence are as follows: Tregony is said to be mentioned as a port of call in the Duchy of Cornwall Accounts for 1365/66;[29] a ship from Tregony is noted in the Exchequer Customs Accounts 1387-89, Account of Prisage (Customs due) of wine wreck in Cornwall;[30] in March 1495 the *Christopher* of Tregony, Master Edward Tromson, landed herring and sprott (sprats?) at Exeter's port of Topsham.[31] It has not been possible to investigate the context of any of the above instances.

Source Notes

1. CRO DDX 256/7

2. CRO G/1590

3. CRO G/225/3

4. CRO F/1/75

5. CRO CF/1/2199

6. Nat.Arch. C131/174/96

7. Nat.Arch. C131/5/33

8. CRO J/1/290

9. Benny, *Cornish Watermills*, 1972.

10. CRO WH/4236/2

11. CRO WH/1/4250

12. CRO WH/1/4251

13. CRO ARD/TER/409

14. Royal Institution of Cornwall HW/28

15. CRO BU/272

16. CRO TRE 6 DDJ 641

17. CRO DDX 256/7

18. Nat. Arch. C1/54/150

19. Devon Record Office 3799 M-O ET/24/8

20. CRO AP/B/155

21. Whetter, *Cornwall in the 17th Century*, 1974

22. CRO G/1657/1-2

23. CRO G/978

24. CRO G/943

25. Charter Rolls 9th Ed. 111.

26. CRO G/235

27. CRO G/258/1-2

28. CRO G/330

29. Duchy Accounts No. 17, m9d

30. Nat.Arch. E122/40/13

31. Devon Heritage Centre, Exeter Port Customs Accounts 1494/95

Abbreviations
CRO – Cornwall Record Office
Nat.Arch. – National Archives

Bibliography

Benny, D.E., *Cornish Watermills*, Bradford Barton (1972).

Bristow, Colin M., *Cornwall's Geology and Scenery*, Cornish Hillside (1996).

Carew, Richard, *Survey of Cornwall*, 1602. Reprint, Tamar Books (2000).

Dart, M., *West Country Mineral Railways*, Middleton Press (2005).

Dury, G., *The Face of the Earth*, Penguin Books (1968).

Environment Agency, *Fal and St Austell Streams Consultation Report*, (1997).

Fogg, Roger, *Cornwall's China Clay Country*, Halsgrove (2011).

Gardiner, Dorothy M., *Early Chancery Proceedings Relating to West Country Shipping, 1388-1493*, Devon and Cornwall Record Society (1976).

Gerrard, Sandy, *The Early British Tin Industry*, Tempus (2000).

Gilson, Peter, *The Upper Fal in old Photographs*, Alan Sutton (1994).

Grigg, Franklin, *Tregony Happenings 1886-1921*, Grigg (2004).

Guthrie, A., *Cornwall in the Age of Steam*, Tabb House (1994).

Halliday, F.E., *A History of Cornwall*, Gerald Duckworth (1959).

Hull, P. L. *The Caption of Seisin in the Duchy of Cornwall*, Devon and Cornwall Record Society (1971).

Kain, R., and Ravenhill, W., Ed. *Historical Atlas of South West England,* University of Exeter Press (1999).

Kowaleski, Dr Maryanne, *The Havener's Accounts of the Earldom and Duchy of Cornwall, 1287-1356,* Devon and Cornwall Record Society (2001).

Mudd, David, *Around and About the Fal,* Bossiney Books (1989).

Pounds, N.J.B., M.A., *Ports and Shipping of the Fal,* Journal of the Royal Insitution of Cornwall, Vo.1, Pt.1. (1946).

Ratcliffe, Jeanette, Ed., *The Fal Estuary Historic Audit,* Cornwall Archaeological Unit, Cornwall County Council (1997).

Stapleton, C., and Pethick, J., *The Fal Estuary, Report to English Nature,* Institute of Coastal Studies, Universiity of Hull (1996).

Weatherhill, Craig, *Cornovia,* Cornwall Books *(1985).*

Whetter, Dr James, *Cornwall in the Seventeenth Century,* Lodeneck Press (1974).

Whitley, H.M., *The Silting up of the Creeks of Falmouth Haven,* Journal of the Royal Institution of Cornwall, VII, pp 12-17 (1881).

Useful Maps
Ordnance Survey Timeline Series, 1813. Map 204, Truro and Falmouth.
Ordnance Survey Explorer Series, Map 105, Falmouth and Mevagissey.
Ordnance Survey Explorer Series, Map 106, Newquay and Padstow.